Four Essential Loves

Jayne & Mark:

Your friendship is a
gift from the Lord
we will treasure - forever!

Blessings & "hugs"

By His grace & for His
glory!

Brian

II Cor 9:8.

Four Essential Loves

Heart Readiness for Leadership and Ministry

William R. McAlpine

WIPF & STOCK · Eugene, Oregon

FOUR ESSENTIAL LOVES
Heart Readiness for Leadership and Ministry

Wipf & Stock
An Imprint of Wipf and Stock Publishers
199 W. 8th Ave., Suite 3
Eugene, OR 97401
www.wipfandstock.com

ISBN 13: 978-1-62032-402-8
Manufactured in the U.S.A.

Scripture quotations, unless otherwise noted, are from the English Standard Version of the Bible, copyright 2001 by Crossway, a publishing ministry of Good News Publishers.

Contents

Preface

LEADERSHIP WITHIN THE CONTEXT of ministry is a topic that has fostered no small amount of published materials. A wide array of excellent works has been dedicated to what might be considered the more practical dimensions of leadership. These dimensions include goal setting or vision casting, delegation, communication and strategizing, and so on. Without question, knowledge and skills are essential to effectiveness in leadership and ministry. Good intentions, sincerity, and a profound love for the Lord and people are incapable in themselves of rendering a person competent to lead. Leadership skills must consistently be developed and honed. But by the same token, the ability to manage and lead, to administrate and envision in the absence of a personal heart readiness, can and unfortunately often does leave a disconcerting litany of carnage in a leader's wake. Reggie McNeal has accurately and insightfully identified that spiritual leadership is a "work of heart."[1]

Over the course of three-and-a-half decades, I have had the privilege to serve the church. After serving more than fifteen years of pastoral ministry in the local church, and just under twenty years of teaching in the academic context of Bible college and seminary, I have come to the conclusion that an individual's readiness for leadership and ministry cannot be assessed solely on the basis of academic achievement or by the statistics found in a pastor's or leader's annual report.

As one who has the delightful privilege of training women and men for ministry in the church and society at large, and who continues to enjoy mentoring young men who have moved on to embrace God's calling on their lives, I am deeply committed to the development of leaders who are already taking the church into the future. But if our main or sole focus in all of these endeavors and privileges associated with mentoring and training individuals is the acquisition of skill and knowledge, then we will invariably

---

1 McNeal, *A Work of Heart.*

shortchange those in the sphere of our influence, and potentially those people who they in turn will lead.

But I must stress that my concern in this whole matter is not limited to those individuals in what we sometimes refer to as vocational ministry or leadership positions. I am as equally committed to assisting lay leadership. Whether leading a small group, a finance committee, serving on an elders' or deacons' board, or leading a team of several pastors, spiritual leadership in any capacity that is motivated by a desire to be engaged in the work of God's kingdom demands a heart readiness that is foundational to all essential knowledge and skill sets. To appoint or elect a person to a leadership or ministry position on the basis of one dimension, while ignoring or even minimizing the others, is to court disaster. Unfortunately all too often leadership teams feel the pressure of having too many vacant positions and not enough able and willing people to fill them. This can result in premature appointments of leaders in any number of situations. Heart readiness by itself ("he has such a good heart") in the absence of a recognized level of proficiency and knowledge will certainly contribute to the frustration of even the best intentions and well laid plans. By the same token, leaders whose business or administrative acumen and experience are devoid of a deep love for the Word of God, for Christ's church, for oneself, and for one's neighbor, including and in particular those who have not begun to develop a relationship with Christ, will, like a boat in shallow water, run aground at some critical point.

The motivation behind this book is intensely practical. It is driven by the question, what qualities are nonnegotiable prerequisites for effectiveness in ministry and leadership? While embracing the significance of knowledge and skill as essential to effective leadership and ministry, I am also convinced that these dimensions must be rooted in that which is less quantifiable, namely *heart readiness.*

The relationship between the elements of heart readiness and essential knowledge and skills can be illustrated through the metaphor of a boat on a river. Leadership skills, like a vessel on a river, are essential in moving a man or woman toward the destination of vocational or ministry effectiveness. But heart readiness is much like the river itself: the water that keeps that vessel from running aground. To a certain degree, skills can be taught, practiced, and honed; and knowledge can be acquired with discipline and hard work. But heart readiness is beyond the capacity of any human to manufacture. Heart readiness is possible only through a supernatural work of God's grace, and that grace is available only as we enter and grow in a relationship with God in which we love him with all we are—heart, soul, mind, and strength.

C. S. Lewis, in his seminal work *The Four Loves*, has furnished us with superlative insights into the many nuances and variegated expressions of love.[2] As such, we need not revisit those details in this book. Rather, the intent of this book is to establish and illustrate how leadership in ministry demands loving the right objects in the right way for the right reasons. Beginning with Jesus' response to the question, "Which command is the most important of all?" (Mark 12:28), we will explore what it looks like in a ministry-leadership context to love God with one's entire being. Growing out of that foundational love, I have identified and developed four essential loves that constitute heart readiness for ministry and leadership. Those four loves are the following: love for *God's Word*, love for *Christ's church*, love for *one's neighbor*, and love for *oneself*. The intent of considering self-love as the last of the four in this book is not to present it as the least important, the bottom rung on the love ladder. More will be said on this in chapter 5. For now, suffice it to say that any attempt to prioritize the four loves here would frustrate or limit meaningful life application. All four loves have their unique challenges and all four are of equal importance in the life of the leader in ministry.

There is a mutually affective relationship between our wholehearted love for the Lord and the other four essential loves. That is, our love for God not only motivates and energizes our love for the church, his Word, our neighbor, and ourselves, but the reverse is also true. Genuine, growing love in these four areas of love can and will deepen and enrich our love for God. However, there is sequence, there is an order in this sense; wholehearted love for the Lord must precede all of the four essential loves. To borrow the illustration of the vine and the branches that Jesus used in John 15 to convey to his disciples how critical it was for them to dwell in him, our love for the Lord is like the vine out of which our love for the Word, the church, our neighbor, and ourselves must grow. Just as the fruit that is born by the branches is, in fact, a demonstration of the life and nature of the vine, our four essential loves are to be demonstrations of our deep- rooted, ever-growing love for the Lord. In other words, we should have ready access into

---

2. Two excellent works that address the subject of love in a much more detailed and thoughtful way than can be included here are C. S. Lewis's *The Four Loves* and Sondra Wheeler's *What We Were Made For: Christian Reflections on Love*.

the nature and depth of our love for the Lord through witnessing our love for God's Word, Christ's church, our neighbor, and ourselves.

Although I acknowledge that there is obvious application of these truths to all Christ followers, this book is focused on the life of the Christian leader in any ministry context. Much of the content in the following pages has been refined through God's marvelous grace in the midst of my own attempts in leadership—good, bad, and ugly—and have been enriched through the examples of the men and women through whose leadership I have seen all of these essential loves expressed.

Each chapter in this book concludes with a short series of questions and suggestions both for group discussion and for personal reflection. It is my hope that the content in each might foster some robust interaction within leadership groups, and provide an opportunity for meaningful reflection and application on a personal level. I would be delighted to hear how or if this has been beneficial to you as leadership teams or as individuals. Any suggestions, comments, or interaction with any of the material in the following pages would also be gratefully received at bmcalpine@ambrose.edu.

One practical note: I have footnoted many passages of Scripture referred to throughout each chapter. I strongly encourage the reader not to be in a hurry to rush through each chapter, but instead take the time to look up each passage and read the context in which it is found.

Finally, I offer this work with the genuine desire to see both the church of Christ strengthened and Christ himself made large through the lives of men and women who are encouraged and enabled to lead with a heart that is ready; a heart that loves God with their whole being manifest in a love for the Word, for the church, for their neighbor, and for themselves.

By his grace and for his glory!

ACKNOWLEDGMENTS

As soon as one steps into the waters of acknowledgment a wave of fear that someone will be missed inadvertently begins to roll in. However, that must not prevent my attempt to at least thank some people. There are so many men and women who have contributed unknowingly to this present work. These people represent an array of leadership styles and possess varying degrees of knowledge and skill, but who all have profoundly impacted my life through their consistent demonstration of heart readiness in their leadership and ministry. When I think of a whole-hearted, all-consuming love for the Lord that flowed into a profound love for the Word and for the church, that became a passionate love for lost people, that inspired incredible sacrifice, I am thankful for my parents, Rev. George and Frances McAlpine. They are now in glory and I still miss them. I am also grateful for a handful of pastors who took a risk in hiring me as their assistant, Rev. John A. Robb and Rev. Arnold P. Reimer in particular. Both were strong leaders of conviction, but their ultimate strength was in the way they whole heartedly loved the Lord, his Word, his church, and lost people. I must also thank Dr. Melvin P. Sylvester who was my first district superintendent in what was the Eastern and Central Canadian District of the Christian and Missionary Alliance in Canada, and who later went on to be our denomination's first president in Canada. I had the wonderful privilege of serving as pastor to Mel, his lovely wife Marion, and two of their sons, Dallas and Grant. During his tenure as district superintendent (being responsible for approximately seventy churches from central Ontario through Quebec to the Maritimes), Mel took a week's holiday to lead a small band of ten- to twelve-year-old boys during our Vacation Bible School. Even with the demands of national and international leadership, he modeled then, as he still does to this day, the four essential loves. His willingness to love and lead was an inspiration to me then and continues to inspire me today.

I could and should mention so many others here. Thanks to many of my students from the past twenty years, too many to mention by name, who have shown the promise of these essential loves. Thanks also to my Scripture memory partner, Tim Bergmann, whose passionate love for the Word has motivated him, and through him others, like me, to commit entire books of the Bible to memory.

Even though it goes without saying, but should never go unsaid, the one who has probably paid as much or more than any other person during this whole writing project is the "bride of my youth," the love of my life, and my very best friend, Heather. She leads not from a president's desk or professor's podium (though she could do either with great effect), but from the sanctuary of her daily love-life with the Lord and his Word. I am one profoundly blessed man.

ONE

Loving God with All I Am: Where It All Begins

THIS BOOK IS ABOUT leadership in a ministry context. But it is also a book about love, arguably the most fundamental need or longing experienced by humanity. The following pages demonstrate that love and leadership are not two radically unrelated realities. Indeed, for the Christian leader in ministry they are intrinsically linked. One cannot lead and minister effectively in the absence of a love for God that not only consumes the entirety of the human person but is recognized as the source for every other love. It is, of course, difficult to identify a universally accepted definition or concept of what love is. It would be unwise for me to assume that author and reader are on the same page in every instance in this regard. Therefore, allow me to outline how the word *love* is understood and used throughout this work.

The Illusive Essence of Love

Though difficult to define, love has probably had as much impact on human history as any other phenomenon. Love has probably inspired more songs, novels, and movies than any other topic. I am well aware that in any conversation or consideration about love there may be a tendency to hover in the realm of the ethereal, philosophical, or theological without ever landing on the *terra firma* of everyday life. This is due in part because there are so many ways in which that four-letter word, love, has been dropped into the English language. As a result, it is very easy for us to minimize the significance of love, or to dilute our appreciation for it. For example, consider how often we have heard or made statements ranging anywhere from "I *love* the grandeur of the mountains." or "the vastness of the big prairie sky," or "the serenity of Redwood forest" to "I *love* the hotdogs at Costco," or "I *love* his preaching," or "I *love* teaching that class." Some would suggest that a better way of expressing these kinds of sentiments would be to use terms like, "I thoroughly enjoy, appreciate, am moved by, or simply like." Generally, however, when we use the word love in relation to such things we mean something deeper than merely liking them (with perhaps the exception of the Costco hotdog!). Implicit in this could be that mountains or prairies or forests can move an individual emotionally, even spiritually; they speak to us of the creator God who brought them into being, or they remind us of how small we are in comparison to God's marvelous creation, all of which speaks of much more than liking or appreciation. There is an existential or emotional response similar to what is felt when reunited with a dear friend. To love anyone or anything is to take great delight in being with them.

Romantic love, more than any other love, has been magnified, deified, and granted messianic powers throughout human history. Timothy Keller puts it so well when he says:

> It has always been possible to make romantic love and marriage into a counterfeit god, but we live in a culture that makes it even easier to mistake love for God, to be swept up by it, and to rest all our hopes for happiness upon it.[1]

It is safe to say, however, that little else devastates the human soul as much or more than failed, rejected, or frustrated love. Yet this almost inevitably is what occurs when love for another human being or for any other object is allowed to usurp our love for God. The insatiable need for that love found in the perfect soul mate is driven by a longing for deliverance from that which Adam needed deliverance even before the entrance of sin into human history, namely, aloneness. But when we allow love for any object, activity, or person prominence in our lives, we have committed sin, the sin of idolatry. Tim Keller puts it this way: "Making an idol out of something means giving it the love you should be giving to your Creator and Sustainer."[2] Even the God-ordained love between a husband and wife or between parent and child when allowed to become the main driving force in our life becomes idolatrous. The same must be said of any ministry in which we are privileged to lead. If I get more enjoyment out of my ministry or invest more energy and time in it than I do my relationship with God, I have effectively turned that ministry into an idol. It is for this reason that

---

1. Keller, *Counterfeit Gods*, 24.
2. Keller, *Center Church*, 128.

we must begin this journey together with a careful look at our love for the Lord, that is, the love from which all other loves flow.

One of the questions that may arise at this point is this: can the word *love* be used legitimately in relation to objects outside the realm of human relationship? Scripture would seem to indicate it can. For example, David used the Hebrew word *ahab*, typically translated into the English word "love," numerous times in Psalm 119 to describe his deep feelings for God's law.[3] Solomon, using the same word, admonishes his son not to forsake wisdom but to *love* her.[4] He also speaks of loving discipline and knowledge.[5] These passages and many more provide ample latitude in which love may be reasonably and meaningfully used to describe feelings toward objects beyond the sphere of human relationships.[6]

The focus of this introductory chapter, however, is the love for God that Jesus himself identified as the greatest or foremost commandment. Loving God, of course, is a basic and simple command, right? One could wish that such was the case. Without understanding God's perspective on what loving him means, and what it should look like in the life of a Christ follower in leadership, all that is offered throughout the remaining chapters of this book will prove frustrating at best and meaningless at worst. Loving God with our whole being is where all effective leadership and ministry must begin.

The Command of Love

It would be very difficult to find any Scripture that provides a more incisive picture of what loving God entails than is found in Deuteronomy 6:4–9, a passage referred to as the Shema. It is this passage with which every devout Jew[7] begins and ends his day; and it is this passage to which Jesus himself referred when asked by a religious leader of his day to identify the greatest commandment.[8]

3. Ps 119:97, 113, 119, 127, 159, 163, 165, 167.

4. Prov 4:6.

5. Prov 12:1.

6. This is essential to the second chapter of this book, which is dedicated to our love for the Word of God.

7. Christians are also coming to appreciate the value of orienting their lives with this wonderful passage. See McKnight, *Jesus Creed*, 12.

8. Matt 22:34–40; Mark 12:28–34.

The verb in the phrase "hear, O Israel" is the Hebrew word shema. This formula is not limited, however, to the well-known passage found in Deuteronomy 6:4–9, but is found a total of five times in the book of Deuteronomy.[9] In three of these instances the phrase seems to introduce a call to radical obedience to God's unrivaled rule. Some have suggested that the phrase connotes a sense of urgency or major significance in that the speaker is not only calling for his listeners' attention but is anticipating a positive response. McBride reminds us: "There is, in other words, a strong note of intentionality conveyed by the verb shema whose force in Hebrew must often be rendered in English by "obey," "heed," rather than simply "hear." If one really hears, he will respond in accord with what he has learned."[10] This loyal obedience cannot be coerced, however. It is a matter of personal choice, as was illustrated in Joshua's exhortation to the people of Israel: "And if it is evil in your eyes to serve the Lord, choose this day whom you will serve . . . But as for me and my house, we will serve the Lord."[11]

From the outset, the Shema establishes that God is one, undivided, and furthermore is the *only* one! This declaration was set in stark contrast to the polytheistic culture in which the nation of ancient Israel was situated. Just as Jehovah was one and undivided so must their love for and allegiance to God be undivided.

There are many legitimate entities that, if allowed, can and will demand our loyalty to the point of diminishing our unrivaled, wholehearted love for our God. As mentioned previously, this is the essence of idolatry. On numerous occasions Jesus underscored the necessity of undivided loyalty in the lives of his followers. Jesus emphasized that the priority of his kingdom and righteousness must be sought first.[12] This commanding priority of loving God makes it impossible for a person to serve two masters,[13] and it is from that undivided loyal love that all other loves must flow.

In light of the fact that, according to Jesus, the greatest commandment is to love God with our whole person and the second is to love our neighbor as ourselves, one may ask a simple question: Is it possible for love to be commanded? Such a concept is so foreign to the people of any culture in which love is perceived to be something to "fall into" or that ambushes individuals

9. Deut 5:1; 6:4; 9:1–3; 20:3; 27:9.
10. McBride, "Yoke of the Kingdom." 290.
11. Josh 24:15.
12. Matt 6:33.
13. Matt 6:24.

irresistibly. Such cultures often thus relegate and limit love to the realm of the emotions. But the love that God demands in this "foremost" or greatest command calls for the entirety of our humanness—our intellect, emotion, physical energy, and volition—to be engaged if it is to be acceptable to God and influential in shaping our lives and ministry. In essence *loving God with my whole being is an act of obedience.* Sondra Wheeler puts it this way: "Love is the foundation on which every act of obedience and faithfulness is built, that which makes such acts really good and not merely seemingly good, for without such love even our best acts "profit us nothing" (1 Cor 13:3 KJV)."[14]

This love for God is not just a noble, spiritual ideal for which God's people are to strive, nor is it merely some kind of mystical experience or exercise through which the law is rendered redundant. This love is a duty that is expected to have an existential expression engaging all of our human faculties and capacities.[15] To love God is to obey his commands not out of a suffocating sense of obligation inherent in some form of binding ritual but out of a recognition and acceptance of the love that God has already extended to us. Thus, our obedience to God and his decrees is not driven by fear and its companion, uncertainty, but by love. "Hence the doing of the law, epitomized as the love of God, begins in the heart and embraces the whole man."[16] In this way, the law ceases to be an external imposition and becomes instead an internal source of strength and joy, not written on tablets of stone but on our hearts of flesh.[17]

During my teen years I had ample opportunity to dabble in a wide variety of activities that ran contrary to the standards and lifestyle modeled and expected by my parents. Occasionally I would cave under the persuasive pressures of my peers. But by God's grace, I am grateful that I was never lured into doing things that had potentially serious consequences. Reflecting back on those days I can easily identify one of the most influential forces in my life that helped me resist those pressures. That influence was my love for my mom and dad. My dad was a loving yet stern disciplinarian. I knew that choosing to disregard the fences that he had set up for me came with significant risk, especially if I got caught! However, greater than a debilitating fear of my dad's stern discipline, it was more often a fear

14. Wheeler, *What We Were Made For*, 17.
15. McBride, *Yoke of the Kingdom*, 298.
16. Ibid., 302.
17. Jer 31:31–34.

of hurting my folks, born out of a love for them that kept me and enabled me to obey them. In a similar way, a growing love for God with all that we are can serve as one of our greatest defences against the lures of the enemy of our souls.

For many of us, part of our struggle in loving God this way is that we perceive him as a remote and abstract entity, such as the United Nations. We may not know much about the United Nations, and in fact may pay very little attention to it, but we are glad in a broad sense to know it is there! We assume that it is doing some good in and for the world, but on a personal level our engagement with the United Nations or even conversations about it are so infrequent that for all intents and purposes our lives could likely carry on fine without it. The only possible exception might be during a time of crisis that threatens our own personal or national safety. This perception is a far cry from a love that engages heart, soul, mind, and strength.

Loving God with All I Am

What does it mean, then, to love God with one's *heart, soul,* and *might*?[18] When we turn to Mark's account of an exchange Jesus had with one inquisitor we find the added phrase: "and with all your mind."[19] It is also interesting that Jesus adds Leviticus 19:18 to the Judaistic Shema by saying, "And the second is like it—love your neighbor as yourself."

In the account provided by Mark, it is a teacher of the law (NIV) or scribe (ESV) who presents Jesus with the question, "Which commandment is the most important of all?" It is essential that we understand the context in which this question is asked. A teacher of the law or scribe was trained for and devoted to the proper and meaningful interpretation of the law. His life was immersed in the law that encompassed more than the Decalogue, or Ten Commandments, and included the 613 statutes that had been crafted over time. Rabbis had established 365 prohibitions and 248 positive commands, all of which were to influence appropriate conduct. In light of this it is safe to assume that, reflective of the religious culture of his day, the man was asking the question out of a "works-righteousness understanding of the law and the keeping of its commandments."[20]

---

18. Deut 6:5.
19. Mark 12:30.
20. Wessel, "Mark," 737.

Jesus is not being asked to identify or prioritize one of the Ten Commandments as the most important of all in a technical, sterile sense. Rather, he is being asked what is the epitome or foundational beginning of the law.[21] He is being asked to translate the Law out of the complex, theoretical realm into an accessible, meaningful application to life. In other words, which commandment provides an all-encompassing principle that weaves all the statutes of the law, whether ritual or ethical, "weighty" or "light,"[22] into a coherent paradigm for life? Jesus' answer seems to assume that this was the intent behind the question, as evidenced in his summary statement (vs. 31): "There is no other commandment greater than these." Reducing 613 commands down to the two found Deuteronomy 6:4 and Leviticus 19:18 was an unprecedented move on Jesus' part. As far as we can tell from early sources, there is no indication that the combination of these two commands (loving God and loving our neighbor) appeared in any other teaching prior to Jesus.

Heart, Soul, Mind, and Strength

Historically, a number of interpretive approaches to this passage have been offered. These approaches range from those that have attached unique significance to each particular aspect mentioned to those that consider the words *heart, soul, mind,* and *strength* to be a summation of the whole person. For example, early Old Testament exegetes chose to distinguish these elements as distinct though complementary expressions of love for God. Loving God with *all one's heart* referred to an undivided loyalty comprised primarily of the human will; whereas loving God *with all one's soul* (life) described a commitment to God, even to the point of death, should that be necessary. Some would suggest that to love the Lord with all our soul (*nephesh*) means to love him as long as we have breath, to the end of one's life. The term *nephesh* is also used in terms of one's desires or appetites.[23] When the Psalmist declares[24] "To you, O Lord I lift up my soul," he is declaring that just like the beak of a newly hatched bird opens upward in the anticipation of being fed by its mother, so too he lifts his soul (*nephesh*) to God who alone can satisfy his deepest appetites and desires. *Strength* was

21. McBride, *Yoke of the Kingdom,* 281.

22. See McKenna, *Communicator's Commentary,* 252.

23. See Janzen, "Claim of the Shema," n.10, p. 252.

24. Ps 25:1.

considered by some to mean substance, including wealth and/or property, which was to be available in the service of God. By contrast, early Christian exegetes, who worked primarily with the Greek text,[25] looked at all of these as complementary aspects of our humanity that combined to describe the whole inner person.

In ancient Hebrew thought, the heart was considered the seat or organ of the intellect and the soul, the home of desires and affections. Likewise, when we come to Mark's account of Jesus' response to the scribe's question, the word heart (*kardia*) "is the source and seat of deliberative thought. As the center of the personal life, it is the sphere not only of the passions and emotions, but of the thoughts and intellectual processes, at least so far as they go to make up the moral character."[26]

The expression "with all your heart and all your soul" is not found exclusively in the Shema language of Deuteronomy 6. The expression is found seventeen times in the Old Testament. It is an adverbial phrase that can also be stated with the term "wholeheartedly"; and it is descriptive of the assumed attitude any person entering into a covenant was to possess, that is, without reservation.

God's command in the Shema and its threefold repetition in the Synoptic Gospels leave no room to doubt the importance of our mind in our service, devotion, and commitment to the Lord. Loving God with our minds does not preclude asking tough questions about or because of our faith. This command will, instead, encourage us into the public arena of intellectual exchange where ideas can be shared, assessed, and challenged, hopefully in the absence of personal assault.

Passion must not be divorced from reason. Loving God is not relegated to the emotive dimension of our person; it also entails the disciplines and rigors of intellectual pursuit. It involves more than passion and feeling; it entails thinking and doing as well. Having said this, reason should never be allowed to eclipse the heart. Loving God with our minds moves us beyond mere intellectual apprehension. Loving God moves us into a willingness to have our minds affected, indeed changed, into the mind of Christ.[27] This willingness demands us to revisit and if need be relinquish our settled mindsets and cherished biases. There is no risk in loving God with our

---

25. Here we are referring to the Gospel accounts in particular.

26. Swete, *Commentary on Mark*, 35.

27. Phil 2:5.

minds when confronted with the truth of God's word. There is only risk in refusing to do so.

Those of us in ministry leadership roles must not underestimate the intellectual capacity of those we lead. They, too, can think deeply. As Christians we have made our feelings and our passionate convictions about various issues abundantly clear. Even so, some would question our ability to present the intellectual rationale behind our passion in a compelling manner. Halford E. Luccock suggests in his commentary on the Gospel of Mark that just as Muslims remove and leave their shoes outside before entering the Mosque, too many Christians leave their minds outside any meaningful dialogue.[28] This observation does not deny the existence and influence of brilliant Christian minds. But it is difficult to deny the fact that many Christian young people have been discouraged from pursuing a university education for fear that they will be intellectually bullied out of their heart passion for and faith in Christ.[29]

Loving God with our heart, mind, soul, and strength leaves no room for any gap between knowledge and action or between passion and reason. Loving God in the way described in the Shema calls for an integration of heart and mind, of soul and strength. It is a holistic love that resists the dissecting of our humanness and, in particular, the expressions of our love for the Lord. This is a love that thinks, feels, and acts. This means there is nothing about me that will not serve as a vehicle of my love for God. Loving God involves the participation of the whole person, not just the soul or heart, but all of me: body, soul, heart, and mind. Notice also God's expectations are not expressed in fractional terms but in superlative terms: "you shall love the Lord your God with *all* your heart, and with *all* your soul and with *all* your might." This is a comprehensive command that Jesus reiterates with the inclusion of "*all* your mind."[30]

For many, loving God consists fundamentally of an outward expression evidenced in compliance to certain regulations or rituals. But it was for mere external observances that God criticized his own people. Let us recall what God said through his prophet Isaiah: "Because this people draw near with their mouth and honor me with their lips, while their hearts are far

28. See in Buttrick, *Interpreter's Bible, Vol. 7*, 848.

29. An excellent book on the Christian mind is James Emery White's *A Mind for God*, which includes two very helpful appendices that consist of three suggested reading lists and other resources for learning and the development of a Christian world view.

30. Mark 12:29–31.

from me, and their fear of me is a commandment taught by men . . ."[31] In the New Testament the apostle Paul admonishes Timothy to avoid those he described as "having the appearance of Godliness, but denying its power."[32]

Loving God in this way is challenging even for those who have been known for their devotion to and love for God. Jesus' personal letter to the Church in Ephesus, preserved for us in the writings of the Apostle John,[33] includes a severe indictment for the church members' inability to maintain and preserve their first love, the love that should take preeminence over any and all other loves. This was a church that the living, glorified Christ praised for their patient endurance, their refusal to tolerate evil, and their knowledge of and commitment to pure doctrine. Yet somehow they "abandoned the love you had at first."

This all-encompassing love for God must precede and be the wellspring from which all holy living must come. John Wesley declared it this way: "we must love God before we can be holy at all; this being the root of all holiness."[34] For him, love for God subordinates and orders all other loves. This is a point that we must clearly understand and embrace in order to make sense of the remaining chapters of this book. We must avoid the danger of allowing any other legitimate love to usurp the position of our "first love." It is alarmingly easy, to the point of being natural, for us to allow love for God to be eclipsed, at times imperceptibly, by a love for the word, for the church, for our neighbor and, of course, for ourselves. Yet love for God that does not spill over into these other loves is a truncated aberration, a flawed replica that ultimately will have little or no influence in making our hearts ready for ministry. Love for God that encompasses our entire being must be the headwaters from which all other loves flow and have their source.

Language similar to what we find in the Shema appears when Israel, being called to return to the Lord, had demonstrated either an inability or unwillingness to love the Lord and him alone. In Deuteronomy 30, for instance, we find the phrase "with all you heart and with all your soul" repeated three times in God's call to repentance and his willingness to forgive his people. God calls them, first to "obey his voice . . . with all your heart

---

31. Isa 29:13.

32. 2 Tim 3:5.

33. Rev 2:1–7.

34. Wesley, *Works*, Vol 5, 115.

and all your soul."[35] Then in verse 6 we read, "And the Lord your God will circumcise your heart and the heart of your offspring, so that you will love the Lord your God with all your heart and with all your soul, that you may live." Finally, in verses 9 and 10 of the same chapter we are told, "For the Lord will again take delight in prospering you, as he took delight in your fathers, when you obey the voice of the Lord your God, to keep his commandments and his statutes that are written in this Book of the Law, when you turn to the Lord your God with all your heart and with all your soul."

According to the Shema language, our love for God is to be the love to which all other loves are to be subservient; it is to be unreserved and unqualified in its commitment to the covenant and to God himself. The fact that Israel was expected, indeed commanded, to bring the Shema intentionally into the beginning and the end of each day[36] indicates this was not meant merely to be pious gesture. Rather, this love was meant to provide an orientation for life. It is these words, enshrined in the Shema, that are contained in the Mezuzah that is found on the doorpost of Jewish homes. In the same way, leadership and ministry within the body of Christ and in the world must be oriented like a compass to the true north of a wholehearted love for the Lord. As McBride reminds us, "The true servants of Yahweh are those who, having confessed his preeminent kingship over their own lives, accord their fellow subjects the same worth they themselves have received in abundance."[37]

Jesus' summary statement, in which he states that the whole law and prophets hang on these two commandments, in no way denies or minimizes the significance of the Torah or Law. Rather, Jesus asserts that the fulfillment or the outworking of the law in our personal lives is measured in love.

No facet of our human person is to be left unengaged in our love relationship with the Lord. Nor is that relationship to become insular or isolated from our relationships with others in our world. It is almost as though Jesus was saying that the litmus test of our love for God is the love we have for our neighbor. There is reason to believe that the Pharisees of Jesus' day had managed to separate love for God as a "weighty" issue from love for one's neighbor as a "light" issue, or at least of lower priority to

35. Deut 30:2.

36. Deut 6:7.

37. McBride, "Yoke of the Kingdom," 282.

love for God.[38] Jesus undermines such a dichotomy by fusing the two into one. That is why Jesus says, "There is no greater commandment (singular) than these (plural)."[39] The implication of this truth is that the four loves of heart readiness are not four unrelated expressions of love lived out on four isolated planes of human existence. Rather, these loves are all intricately woven into a single tapestry.

The scribe's response to Jesus' answer provides another insight important to our consideration:

> And the scribe said to him, "You are right, Teacher. You have truly said that he is one, and there is no other besides him. And to love him with all the heart and with all the understanding and with all the strength, and to love one's neighbor as oneself, is much more than all whole burnt offerings and sacrifices."[40]

The scribe's response provides strong evidence that he was fully aware of the essential significance of the opening words in the Shema ("the Lord our God, the Lord is one"), that they were much more than a preamble or introduction. These opening words constituted a declaration of one's acceptance of God's supreme rule as foundational to all other aspects of the law. A declaration of this kind of loyalty was to be embodied in a life of obedience to the commands invested in God's law; and it was to be an obedience fostered by wholehearted love for God and love for one's neighbor. Because love for our neighbor serves as the focus of chapter 4 in this book, at this juncture we will not develop this essential element of love.

That last phrase in the scribe's response ("and to love one's neighbor as oneself, is much more than all whole burnt offerings and sacrifices"), which seemed to relegate burnt offerings and sacrifices to a secondary position, would have shocked Jesus' audience profoundly. Such a statement would possibly distance the scribe from his religious colleagues. Yet this statement is an echo from the teaching of Old Testament prophets such as Hosea[41] through whom God declared, "For I desire mercy, not sacrifice and acknowledgment of God rather than burnt offerings." Furthermore, this statement demonstrates an understanding that I believe to be essential to effectiveness in leadership and ministry—an understanding that heart

---

38. See Wessel, "Mark," 736.

39. Mark 12:31.

40. Mark 12:32–33.

41. Hos 6:6.

readiness, that is wholehearted love for God and for one's neighbor, must be foundational to any and all other loves or accomplishments, skills, or knowledge. As a teacher of the law, the scribe had been steeped in the ritualistic and ethical intricacies of law, and yet he found something in Jesus' teaching that enabled him to see that there was something of greater value than ritualistic sacrifice and offerings, namely wholehearted love for God and love for one's neighbor. In Jesus' assessment this was a wise response.[42]

The Shema in the Life of Jesus

The life of Jesus himself provides the best lens through which to sharpen our focus on what it looks like to wholeheartedly love God and our neighbor. Reflecting on the meaning and significance of this twofold command through the grid of even the highest human virtue or example is going to leave one with a watered-down essence of what these words entail. How then did Jesus love the Father, and how did he demonstrate love for his neighbor?

Jesus' Love for His Father

Simply put, Jesus' love for the Father was lived out in complicit obedience to the Father's will, even though such love cost him dearly. Matthew recounts the intensity of Jesus' struggle with the Father's will that, for him who knew no sin, included being made of sin so that we might be made whole in the righteousness of God.[43] In a rather awkward conversation, in which his disciples were unabashedly discussing who should be the greatest in the kingdom, Jesus reminded them that the Father's will for the Son of Man was not to be served but to serve and give his life as a ransom for many.[44] It was clearly his love for the world that moved God to provide his Son, the Lord Jesus, as the perfect and only acceptable sacrifice on our behalf.[45] But as much or more than his love for the world, it was Jesus' love for the Father that kept him on the cross. Wholehearted love for his Father—heart, soul, mind, and strength—moved Jesus to extravagant, inconceivable ex-

42. Mark 12:34.
43. Matt 26:36–44.
44. Mark 10:45.
45. John 3:16.

pressions of love. And the Father's announcement of his love for his Son at Jesus' baptism, "You are my beloved son; with you I am well pleased,"[46] was a public, definitive statement of the love that had existed within the Trinity throughout all eternity.

Yet when we consider the Gospels carefully we are confronted with the fact that Jesus did not demonstrate his wholehearted love for the Father through nonstop, frenetic activity and service. Jesus incorporated a pattern into his ministry in which he spent unhurried, unhindered time alone with his Father.[47] These times were not merely efforts to get away from people; they were times when he made the effort to find rest with his Father. It was a habit he encouraged his disciples to engage as well. "Then, because so many people were coming and going they did not even have a chance to eat, he said to them, 'Come with me by yourselves to a quiet place and get some rest.'"[48] Jesus' ministry demonstrated that there is virtually no truth or substance in the adage "the need constitutes the call." Although I appreciate the basic sentiment of a statement like this, I would still argue that the need does *not* constitute the call; *obedience* constitutes the call. I remember hearing a speaker in chapel once declare, "I'd rather burn out for Jesus than rust out!" Either way, friend, you're out! There were times in Jesus' ministry when he walked away from people who needed to grapple with the claims of the good news, whose souls needed to be saved, whose bodies needed healing, and whose spirits needed deliverance! Why? He knew he also needed to spend time intentionally in the presence of his Father.

It is easy for us to become so consumed with serving our God, and consider that investment of time and energy as the best demonstration of our love for him, that we create little or no time simply to be *with* him. Mark tells us that Jesus appointed the twelve not only to preach the good news of the kingdom and to have authority to drive out demons, but first of all, to be *with* him.[49] Leadership in ministry is demanding, to say the least. Carving out time to simply be with the Lord can often prove to be one of the most frustrating challenges leaders experience. Yet loving God with our heart, soul, mind, and strength absolutely demands that ministry leaders do just that. In fact, some readers, right now may be feeling those annoying

46. Mark 1:11.

47. Consider the following examples: Matt 4:1–11; 14:13, 23; 26:36– 46; Mark 1:35; 6:31; Luke 5:16; 6:12.

48. Mark 6:31.

49. Mark 3:13–15.

twinges of self-induced guilt. You may be saying to yourself something like, "I know I really should be spending more time alone with the Lord. But I must devote my attention to this building program, or this planning retreat, or this new teaching series, or these weddings and premarital coaching sessions, or these all-consuming part-time graduate studies . . ." (need I add any more?). There is no redemptive value in that guilt. Rather, my heart's desire is to encourage as many as possible to discover the deep, liberating joy that our loving God wholeheartedly can bring to our personal life and ministry.

Jesus' teaching on the greatest commandment has profound implications for every Christ follower, regardless of his or her station in life. But its application is of particular significance within the realm of leadership in ministry. I believe that those individuals in ministry leadership positions face obstacles to loving the Lord wholeheartedly that are as great, if not greater, than the average lay person. I vividly remember a conversation with a friend who, shortly after being laid off, started attending the church I was pastoring. Because he had some free time one day, I invited him to join me in some pastoral visitation calls. It was great having him along. Upon our return to the church he made this comment out of the blue: "Boy I envy you, Bill—having all this time just to pray and be with the Lord in his word." It took the fullness of the Spirit and all the grace God gave at that moment to keep me from laughing in his face! At first I thought he was joking, but soon discovered that this was his actual perception of what his pastor did between Sundays!

I am sure many people in ministry positions have fantasized about having the luxury to spend the lion's share of the week to study, pray, meditate, and dig into the word. This was, in fact, the workaday schedule of the American pastor and author A. W. Tozer. Many lives, including my own, have been and continue to be deeply enriched and challenged through the prophetic ministry, writings, and recorded sermons of Tozer. But alas, his was a very special vocation to which very few are called. The vast majority of us in ministry leadership positions find that our time and resources are at the beck and call of numerous stakeholders. We are at the mercy of regular responsibilities and those unannounced walk-ins. Furthermore, we want to be responsible, loving spouses and parents.

I know the frustration that can occur in attempting to find time to be *with* the Lord. But I have also come to believe that loving God with all that I am demands it. Leadership and ministry that is not born out of wholehearted love for God and uncompromising, aggressive love for one's neighbor may enjoy temporary, even impressive and effective results. However, in the long run, the ship will eventually run aground.

Jesus and the Law

The way in which Jesus incorporates the Shema into his response to the inquisitor makes it very clear that his intention was not to reduce or denigrate the law. Wholehearted love for the Lord and love for our neighbor do not displace the law. Rather, according to Jesus, they constitute the foundation upon which all the law and prophets hang.[50] But we must be clear, the twofold command to love God and love our neighbor was more than a mere summary statement of the law and prophets, more than a commandment over which no other commandment could take precedence. The whole law and the prophets, indeed all of Scripture, are founded upon the command to love God and our neighbor to the effect that "the multitude of laws in Scripture are valid inasmuch as and insofar as they embody Jesus' central injunction to love God and neighbor."[51]

An underlying assumption has been present throughout this chapter that needs to be made explicit. Loving God wholeheartedly is fundamentally and absolutely contingent upon a personal and biblically based knowledge of who God is. We must resist the allure of embracing one of any number of "tribal gods," the images of which can easily be informed more by denominational or traditional apparatus than by God's revelation of himself through Christ and in Scripture. I am not advocating a moratorium on creedal statements, as long as such statements are reflective of and replete with Scripture. When we allow ourselves to become more provincial in our concerns about the futures and fortunes of our particular group, or when our orthodoxy is more informed by personal opinion or cultural agendas than by the moorings of Scriptural principle, we effectively cut ourselves adrift in danger of being "tossed to and fro by the waves and carried about by every wind of doctrine, by human cunning, by craftiness in deceitful schemes."[52] Without question, "great is the mystery of godliness,"[53]

---

50. Matt 22:40.

51. Gardner cited in Yoder, *Take this Word to Heart*, 128.

52. Eph 4:14.

53. 1 Tim 3:16.

but the essence of who God is and what loving him entails has not been left to human speculation.

What would it be like if all of us who are privileged to minister in any capacity, both within the church and beyond, were to lead like King Josiah? Josiah is described in 2 Kings 23:25 as follows: "Neither before nor after Josiah was there a king like him who turned to the Lord as he did—with all his heart and with all his soul and with all his strength, in accordance with all the law of Moses." Can you imagine? More practically, leaders in ministry need to ask this question: In terms of my influence as a leader, what is the greatest thing I can do? What is most important, foremost? We find the answer in Jesus' response to his inquisitor—love God wholeheartedly and love you neighbor as yourself.

Jesus' take on what is of foremost importance reminds us that, in God's economy, the greatest contribution we can make has nothing to do with accomplishment but has everything to do with relationship—first with God, then with our neighbors. This essential truth brings into bold relief the vital foundation of understanding and experiencing the wonder of a wholehearted love for God. Without that love, all other legitimate loves are in danger of running aground in the shallow waters of self-effort and self-entitlement.

In whatever capacity you may find yourself privileged to serve as a leader, let a wholehearted love for God be the compass that orients your every decision, every response, every conversation so that you can say, "I am doing this at this time in this way first and foremost because I love the Lord my God with all my heart, soul, mind, and strength; I am doing this because this is the most authentic expression of how much I love my neighbor. And I'm doing this not because I *have* to but because I *get* to."

Over the years, God has allowed men and women to discover and develop paradigms and principles of leadership that have served the church wonderfully.[54] But as cultural, sociological, and theological landscapes continue to morph, many such principles can become dated and begin to run out of shelf life, or they are proven effective in one context yet are woefully dysfunctional in another. There is a principle, however, the effectiveness of which is transtemporal and transcultural. This principle has maintained its influence across the borders of time, location, personality, and circum-

54. I have benefited much and still apply insights gained through my attendance at Leadership Summits developed by Bill Hybels and the team at Willow Creek Community Church.

stance. It is what could be referred to as the Shema principle of loving God with all I am. And it is here that all effectiveness in leadership and ministry begins.

For Group Discussion:

1. In what ways could/should whole hearted love for God be evident with a local congregation?

2. In what ways is the congregation of which you are a part doing well in this regard? In what ways do you think improvement might be necessary?

For Personal Reflection:

1. What aspects of your personal life and ministry would you say provide good indicators of your love for God?

2. What potential idols do you see in your own life right now that could possibly usurp God as the supreme object of your delight?

3. What kinds of activities are you doing presently that will enhance or cause your love for God to grow?

Prayer: *Oh Lord, my God, I have so much to learn about what it means to love you! When I consider the depth of your love for me, indeed for the world, I am embarrassed by how poverty-stricken my love for you is by comparison. But I choose this day not to wallow in my shallow inabilities and allow myself instead to be embraced by the wonder of the fact that you do love me. How incredible! I choose to love you this day with my whole heart, soul, mind, and strength, recognizing that to do so is only possible by your grace and for your glory. In Jesus' name, Amen.*

TWO

Love for God's Word

Why Start Here?

IT IS POSSIBLE THAT some readers may question my use of the word *love* with respect to something that is impersonal, namely, the *word of God*—the Bible. These readers may be more comfortable with other expressions, such as what we find in Psalm 1:1–2: "but his *delight* is in the law of the Lord and on his law he meditates day and night." These readers might agree that it is possible to take great delight or experience enjoyment in an object or place but not to love them. This is not an uncommon point of view, for many of us have been conditioned to believe that love is reserved for the realm of personal relationship. For these readers, David might provide inspiration for using the word *love* to describe the abstract. As we explored in the previous chapter, David's own attitude toward the word of God, as demonstrated in Psalm 119, is one of love. At least six times he uses the word *delight*, indeed the same word used here in the example of Psalm 1. But we also find at least six instances in which David uses the word *love*. For example, verse 97: "Oh how I *love* your law," verse 113: "I hate the double-minded, but I *love* your law," verse 127: "Therefore I *love* your commandments above gold, above fine gold," verse 159: "Consider how I *love* your precepts." Then David expresses it emphatically in verse 167: "My soul keeps your testimonies; I *love* them exceedingly." There is little or no question that, for David, the law of God was a source of incredible delight. In fact, the word *delight* used in these Psalms and elsewhere refers to that which makes a person happy or, even more significantly, that which is a person's chief desire.

Why should we consider our love for the word of God immediately following a chapter on loving God with our whole being? Why not love for the church or love for lost people? In the preface of this book, I mentioned that the order of this book's chapters has not been prioritized by order of importance, though the placement of this particular chapter might be the exception to that claim. After all, other than God's self-revelation in the person of his Son, the Lord Jesus Christ, there is no greater revelation of who God is, who we are as a human race, and what he has done and is doing on our behalf, than what we find in Scripture, the word of God.

Through my years of service as a pastor and now as a professor in a Christian university, I have gotten the sense that our society has shifted in attitude toward Scripture. The fact that biblical literacy has decreased persistently over the past several decades is beyond dispute. Explanations or reasons for this disconcerting trend remain unclear. But we do know this: "We have more excellent information available than any previous generation and, no doubt, far less than the generations to come, and yet all indicators are suggesting that the average church attendee knows less Scripture than their grandparents did."[1] This trajectory is not only evident among the masses on the street; it seems to be alarmingly similar within the Christian community at large. Furthermore, this decrease in biblical literacy is not only present among the laity, it appears to be creeping into the clergy as well.

Biblical illiteracy in the Global North is not indicative of limited access to Scripture. Far from it. Advances in technology have made it possible for us to carry around more than a dozen full text versions of Scripture on our smartphones! By and large biblical illiteracy in the Western world is a matter of choice; people are simply choosing not to read or study Scripture as much. Why is that? There are several possibilities, obviously, but I would suggest the following key contributing factors.

New and Increased Addictions

Social and medical scientists have identified an increase in sources of addictions that were completely unknown to my grandparents' generation.[2] For example, social networking, video gaming, and Internet browsing have

1. McAlpine, "Biblical Illiteracy and the Technological Tsunami," 17.

2. See Montag et al. "Internet Addiction and Personality in First-person Shooter Video Gamers." *Journal of Media Psychology*, 2011; Vol. 23(4):163–173.

been shown to have an addictive grip over more and more people—children, adolescents, and adults alike. The increase of discretionary time that has accompanied the shrinkage of the average work week is often quickly consumed with "Facebooking" "'tweeting" and online gaming. The impact of these kinds of activities and involvements are already causing concern among psychologists and other professionals. Ellen Toronto's insightful article provides the following observation:

> While greatly facilitating ease of interaction across time and geographic boundaries, the virtual world presents an unreal environment comprised of instant connection and gratification. Online encounters are employed as seemingly fulfilling alternatives to "live person" relationships. Our culture has enthusiastically embraced this surrogate reality in the form of online journals, chat rooms, and gaming, as well as Internet pornography and sexual solicitation. It has become a significant part of modern society and will undoubtedly continue to do so as new generations find ever-innovative ways to integrate it into daily life. Yet we are already aware that excessive preoccupation with the virtual world may prove disruptive both to productive functioning and the development of satisfying relationships. Phrases such as "Internet addiction" have already entered the lexicon and refer to behaviors that are similar to addictions to drugs and alcohol, resulting in academic, social and occupational impairment.[3]

What Dr. Toronto has identified as a disruptive influence—that the addictions of the virtual world seem to be impairing the development of satisfying relationships in the real world—I would suggest is equally significant with respect to a person's love for the word of God.

Absence Makes the Heart Grow Colder

The old adage that suggests that fondness increases with distance or absence simply does not hold true when it comes to our love for Scripture. Whether it is an addictive involvement in the latest technology, or participation in the seemingly ever-increasing menu of leisure activities, *or* an over-involvement in a local church (which I do believe is possible), the less time we make available for exposing our hearts and minds to Scripture, the less likely our love for the word is going to grow. Love of any kind calls

3. Toronto. "Time Out of Mind" *Psychoanalytic Psychology*, 117.

for an investment of time. If I truly love the word it should not be a chore for me to spend time in it. Almost certainly, when fondness for the word wanes, a questioning of its veracity will not be far behind.

Has God Said?

During my undergrad studies in the 1970s most debates on Scripture came from three adversarial positions. There would be one student who believed that Scripture was intrinsically the word of God (an Evangelical); another who took a more flexible stance on Scripture (non-Evangelical); and someone from what was called the Liberal camp (atheist or agnostic). However, it is my experience that in today's classroom exchanges of this nature do not always volley across the Evangelical/non-Evangelical/Liberal divides exclusively. Opponents on this issue not uncommonly live in the same camp, at least when it comes to other issues. In other words, people who embrace a common belief in the salvific work of Christ through his death and resurrection have historically shared a common loyalty to the veracity and authority of Scripture. Such is no longer inevitably the case. It is difficult to identify specific causes of this intriguing shift. I would suggest that an approach to Scripture that is primarily academic and that posits Scripture as a peer among many other works of good literature, deserving careful study and scrutiny, certainly provides the latitude for such change of mindset.

There are two fallouts of this development. Each has the potential to undermine people's love for the word of God. First, in today's world Scripture has been called in question through the intense scrutiny of those who once were but no longer are convinced of its authoritative reliability. My concern is not for Scripture itself. (Centuries of assaults against it have only proven its ability to sustain itself—the Bible does not need us to defend it.) I am more concerned for seekers and Christ followers who may be persuaded to look elsewhere for answers to life's questions. Second, and equally disturbing, is our tendency to allow debates to downgrade Scripture to a focal point of discussion or a mere object of study.

The Reliability of the Word of God

To what exactly was David referring in the above passages from Psalms? When David spoke of the *law*, most scholars would agree that he was not thinking solely of the Ten Commandments, or what are now the first five books of the Old Testament. Rather, David was referring to God's self-revelation, which of course included the law received on Mt. Sinai. The purpose of the law was not primarily to set the boundaries of appropriate conduct among God's people. Its purpose was and is to reveal the glory of God. God's opening statement, or preamble, to the Decalogue in Exodus 20 is a reminder of his own character. "And God spoke all these words, saying, "I am the Lord your God, who brought you out of the land of Egypt, out of the house of slavery."[4] The law then comes as an extension of God's character. It is not an unreasonable stretch to apply a similar understanding to the word of God, that is, the Bible as we know and possess it now.

Scripture has been the object of numerous assaults. Many attempts at undermining its authority and reliability have been undertaken through the centuries. A recent example is Dan Brown's *The Da Vinci Code*,[5] a work that aroused a crescendo of concern among many churches and fostered numerous series of sermons in response.[6] Christians found themselves having to defend their convictions regarding the reliability of the Bible. Many who took Brown's work beyond the superficial level of mere fiction suggested that other "gospels" (such as those that might have informed the storyline of *The Da Vinci Code*) had been discovered that, in turn, cast the Synoptic Gospels in a dubious light. Some people were willing to believe that the image of Jesus presented in Scripture had been tainted by the personal biases and agendas of the Gospel writers. But 2004, when *The Da Vinci Code* appeared, was not the first time the reliability of Scripture was called into question. In fact, assaults of this nature are ancient. The fall of humankind, as recorded in the creation narrative in the first three chapters of Genesis, began in a questioning of God's word when Satan confronted Adam and Eve with "Did God really say . . . ?"[7]

How are Christians to defend the reliability of the Bible in relation to other sacred writings such as the Qur'an or the Book of Mormon, and on what basis? At the risk of oversimplifying such an important matter, one begins with stating that Scripture is undergirded by a compelling critical mass of ancient manuscripts, some written within decades of the life of Jesus. With all due respect, no other sacred text enjoys the same depth of

---

4. Exod 20:1–2.

5. Brown, *The Da Vinci Code*, 2004.

6. Even so, it is impossible to determine with certainty whether or not Brown's explicit intent was to call into question the authority of the Bible.

7. Gen 3:1.

historical evidence. In addition, how can one be sure that the New Testament Gospels, for instance, are anything more than personal, religious testimony, as Loyola philosophy professor Thomas Sheehan has suggested,[8] and are therefore outside the realm of reliable, objective primary sources? Simply, arguments like Sheehan's ignore or minimize a substantial volume of chronological and archaeological evidence that sustains the accuracy of the Gospel accounts. Passion and conviction do not necessarily or inevitably distort fact. If the Gospel writers are to be discounted on the basis of the passion or faith, which is seen by some to undermine history, then so must accounts written by survivors of the Holocaust or the Killing Fields of Cambodia. That three of the Gospels (Mark, Matthew, and Luke) were written within a single generation of Jesus' life and ministry on Earth provides more than adequate reason to assume an accurate transmission of their accounts.

Our purpose here is not to establish a full-orbed apologetic for the veracity of Scripture, although much excellent material of that nature is readily available. Rather, our purpose here is to underscore the important fact that love for the word of God does not require us to abandon reason, or to fear or avoid honest, thoughtful questions regarding Scripture's reliability. The reliability of the word of God has been tried and tested for centuries. The Holy Spirit not only inspired its writing to begin with, but his supervision throughout its entire history has preserved its authority, sufficiently and completely. Furthermore, love for the word does not require the complete removal of all queries or apparent gaps in our understanding of biblical content. The reliability of Scripture is not contingent upon our ability to explain or even understand it in its entirety. There is still the element of mystery in it that allows us only to "see but a poor reflection in a mirror,"[9] which calls for a response of faith. G. K. Chesterton had this to say about mystery: "As long as you have mystery you have health; when you destroy mystery you create morbidity."[10]

Student or Lover?

I personally have engaged in countless hours of studying God's word. I have also guided hundreds of students in exercises designed to take them deeper

8. Sheehan, *The First Coming*, 6.

9. 1 Cor 13:12.

10. Chesterton, *Orthodoxy*, 24.

in their knowledge of and appreciation for Scripture. The challenge for student and teacher alike is not to approach Scripture primarily as an object of academic pursuit, that is, something only to be studied and mastered. As teachers we dedicate ourselves to assisting students to move toward a level of proficiency in exegetical and hermeneutical skills. Teachers hope that through their guidance students will be able to accurately expose what the authors of Scripture meant when they were inspired to write. This is hard work! Some of us as students of the word thrive on these exercises and are energized by the challenge. Others find the grunt work of learning and applying exegetical and hermeneutical principles to a given text of Scripture frustrating, even daunting. Does the difference in struggle lie in the depth of a person's spirituality? Not necessarily. Does such work manifest a difference in spiritual giftedness? Possibly, but again, not necessarily. Whether or not a person has invested the time, energy, and money into the acquisition of linguistic skills that, in turn, will allow them access to the original languages (Hebrew and Greek) is not the key factor in determining the depth or authenticity of a person's love for Scripture. That said, such skills can play a very important role in an individual's technical readiness to lead a teaching ministry.[11] My point here is this: Not all leaders in ministry are called to a teaching/preaching ministry. But all who lead in any ministry capacity *must* have a profound and growing love for God's word. In fact, I would argue that the absence of this love for the word of God disqualifies a person from effective leadership in ministry at any level in kingdom work.

Over the past several years I have begun my homiletics class by asking students, "Do you consider Scripture primarily to be an authority or a gift?" Every year, without exception, there is a division of the house. A student's response to this question often, but not always, reveals the kind of home and/or church from which he or she hails. The discussion gets even more interesting when I drop a second question into the mix, namely, "What difference does it make? If you see Scripture primarily as an authority, how would that affect your own personal relation to the word? Furthermore, how would your teaching or preaching of the word, and your leadership, reflect this conviction?" I have found that, once again, there is an interesting spread of responses. The purpose of these questions is not to gauge a student's skill or knowledge, nor do I mean to use them to address particular theological or dogmatic issues. These questions are intended to draw out attitudinal responses, and as such set us on the rails for this chapter.

11. Eph 4:11–12.

So what does a person who loves the word of God, or for whom the word of God is his/her chief desire, do in ministry? How will this love for or delight in the word of God play out in our lives? There are, of course, numerous possible answers to this question. These answers depend on a wide array of variables such as personality, spiritual giftedness, and personal circumstance. But for our purposes here I am going to distill two evidences of an authentic, growing love for the word of God. They are biblical meditation and Scripture memorization.

The Person Who Loves the Word Is One
Who Will Meditate on that Word

In both Psalm 1 and 119 there seems to be a clear link between the practice of meditation and the love for or delight in the word and law of God. Unfortunately, we in the West or Global North have a relatively weak grasp of what meditation really is or entails. Scripture is basically silent on the "how" of meditation, and for a legitimate reason: those who originally received Scripture lived in cultures in which meditation was an integral part of the ethos. When David states, for instance in Psalm 1:2, "but his delight is in the law of the Lord and on his law he meditates day and night," those who heard or sung this would very likely know what this meant. That is, they would easily be able to identify with this statement because its sentiment was already a part of their own daily life and worship. We can't say that this is the case in our culture. Many of us have been left to discover the "how" of meditation on our own. If your growing up experiences were like mine, you received very little guidance or instruction specifically on the "how to" but plenty of admonition on the why and the "oughta." Rick Warren gave some of the clearest and best direction on the "how" of meditation when he said, "If you know how to worry, you know how to meditate."

Meditation speaks of unhurried lingering. There are two Hebrew words that translate into the English word "meditate." Interestingly, one is what linguists call onomatopoeia—a word that actually sounds like what is being indicated. (Examples in English are words such as "pop" or "boom.") This Hebrew word is *hagah*, which means a lowing or murmuring. It comes from the root meaning to murmur (in pleasure or anger), and when pronounced it sounds like what is being conveyed. By implication the use of the word evolved to include the ideas of pondering, imagining, mourning, and even studying. The other Hebrew word for "meditation" is *siyach*.

This word means to muse, contemplate, or rehearse in one's mind. Together these words are used just under fifty times in the Old Testament alone.[12]

Historically, people who have heard from the Lord have done so not on account of their unusual talents or sacrifices, but because they carved out time and invested effort in putting themselves in the place where they could hear and listen to that "still small voice." Squeezing God into a fifteen or twenty minute window at the beginning or end of our day is hardly what the Lord has in mind when he insists that we meditate on the law day and night. *Meditation on Scripture is not always convenient, nor is it easy, but it is absolutely essential to leadership effectiveness in any ministry that is to endure for the long haul.*

We do not become proficient in a discipline such as meditation by reading helpful contemporary books on the subject; nor do we gain this skill through the biographies of saints who faithfully devoted themselves to the practice, as beneficial as reading such works may be. Rather we learn to meditate and thus deepen and enrich our love for the word most effectively by doing it, by meditating.

But how do we avoid allowing the word of God to become little more than one of several tools in our ministry kit or weapons in our arsenal or merely the object of analysis and discussion? How do we avoid the danger of transforming the word into an object to be studied and understood while falling shy of embracing it as a living force, a treasure to be cherished? The answer is surprisingly simple: You must love the word with all of your heart, mind, soul, and strength.

It is challenging to love something if you spend time with it only because academic study requires you to do so. Likewise, it's very difficult to love the word if you spend time with it only to prepare for an activity that falls under the realm of your ministerial responsibilities. There is a huge difference between spending time in the word because you *have* to or *ought* to and spending time in the word because you *get* to.

Without for a moment denying the authoritative quality inherent in Scripture, an overemphasis on the authority of Scripture may lend toward an inordinate sense of obligation. David Buttrick suggested:

---

12. Should there be any question with respect to the role of meditation in the life of a leader in ministry, one need only call to mind God's commission of his servant, Joshua. Along with his command to be strong and very courageous, we read in Joshua 1:8 that "This Book of the Law shall not depart from your mouth, but you shall meditate on it day and night, so that you may be careful to do according to all that is written in it. For then you will make your way prosperous, and then you will have good success" (Josh 1:8).

> Of course, we must underscore the word *gift*; we unwrap gifts, delight in gifts, live with gifts, and we are grateful for gifts— "authority" seldom prompts gratitude.[13]

Meditation fosters a delight, a love for the word. But meditation also grows out of that delight. In his book, *Satisfy Your Soul*, Dr. Bruce Demarest writes:

> A quieted heart is our best preparation for all this work of God . . . Meditation refocuses us from ourselves and from the world so that we reflect on God's word, His nature, His abilities, and His works . . . So we prayerfully ponder, muse, and "chew" the words of Scripture . . . The goal is simply to permit the Holy Spirit to activate the life-giving word of God.[14]

Meditation on Scripture born out of a consistently deepening love for that word can profoundly influence and transform a person's heart and spirit. Why is it, then, that so many Christ followers struggle to meaningfully and consistently incorporate this practice into the rhythm of their spiritual journey? I would suggest two key contributing factors. First, within North American Evangelicalism it seems meditation has received, unfortunately, some bad press. The contemplative life has been relegated to the private reserve of New Age practitioners or other traditions outside of the embrace of Orthodox Christianity. This sentiment has progressed to the point that, in the minds of some Evangelicals, meditation is synonymous with New Age and Eastern religions. Indeed, some members of the Evangelical Protestant community are deeply concerned that a recent resurgence of interest in ancient spiritual practices is directing their church dangerously close to the spirituality and mysticism of the Roman Catholic Church.[15] The fact that some members of this faith community practice meditation for reasons beyond scriptural principle is beyond dispute. But this fact in itself is not reason enough to jettison the practice of meditation altogether. Scripture makes it abundantly clear: God expects his people to meditate. To refuse to engage and develop the practice of meditation solely on the basis that others (who represent a religious tradition different from our own) have incorporated this practice into their own spiritual journey is terrible logic.

13. Buttrick, *Homiletic*, 249.

14. Demarest, *Satisfy Your Soul*, 133.

15. See for example Oakland, *Faith Undone*, and Reeves, *The Other Side of the River*.

Such a choice is equivalent to refusing to use twenty dollar bills ever again solely on the basis that there are counterfeit bills in circulation!

The very nature of meditating on Scripture forces us to slow down, to ponder, to reflect. The benefit of doing so is the acquisition of insight. As Solomon testified, "Then I saw and considered it: I looked and received instruction."[16] Such intentional stopping to reflect or contemplate is radically contrary to many of the core values embraced by our fast-food, microwave culture—a culture that is committed to multitasking its way through the day as quickly and efficiently as possible! I have come to believe that life is too short to be in a hurry. A love for God's word that finds expression in unhurried reflection and meditation, listening to God's heartbeat in and through the word, taps us into a deep and powerful resource that is essential to effectiveness in leadership and ministry. As Richard Foster asserts:

> If we hope to move beyond the superficialities of our culture, including our religious culture, we must be willing to go down into the recreating silences, into the inner world of contemplation.[17]

This is not a contemplation that disengages or empties the mind. Rather such contemplation is a disciplined praxis that is securely anchored on the truth of God's revelation in Scripture.

A second challenge to the consistent practice of biblical meditation is that the average Christian today does not know how to engage in meditation in general, and scriptural meditation in particular. The lack of clear biblical teaching on the nature of and need for meditation in the Christian's spiritual journey, coupled with an absence of clear "how to," has fostered an ambivalence and even confusion. Silence is always very difficult to interpret accurately.

This silence essentially leaves many Christians to discover the effectiveness of meditation on their own. The result is a more subjective, overly experiential approach to spirituality, which in turn moves believers away from the security and stability of objective, scriptural moorings.

The question then, is how does one meditate on scripture? There are many excellent resources available that are dedicated to biblical meditation. The following suggestions represent a very short list of elements I have found helpful in developing the meaningful practice of this discipline.

16. Prov 24:32.

17. Foster, *Celebration*, 15.

Location: As much as possible, find a quiet location that is free from distractions such as TV, computers or other electronic devices. Many people find the practice of meditation greatly enhanced by being outdoors, in nature. Others find that distracting and prefer a quiet space in their home or other location. Whatever is most effective for you is the best location.

Timing: Determining the best time for meditating on scripture will depend on an individual's personality (whether a 'morning person' or a 'night owl') and station in life. Mothers of young children and shift workers will have to exercise a significant degree of flexibility recognizing that the same time of day may not be available on a consistent basis. It is essential to be realistic in terms of time parameters. Five minutes likely will be inadequate and unproductive, while trying to maintain an hour or more a day will likely prove frustrating and discouraging.

Length of Passage: I have found prayerfully reading a shorter passage several times over much more beneficial than meditating on a lengthy chapter. Even one verse or a phrase within a verse can often provide a rich resource from which to receive God's word to our heart. Read slowly, sometimes audibly and punctuate the time with seasons of silent attentiveness to what God by his Spirit through his word might be saying to you.

Converse with God: Biblical meditation involves an on-going conversation with the Lord in which we thank him for the splendid treasure of his word, and invite and expect him to speak to us through his word. It entails attaching one's heart and mind to what God has revealed and often fosters an immediate response in which we pray back to him the words we may have just pondered. The vast majority of my times of meditation on scripture will end with a prayer like, "Father, what does this mean for me—today—in my situation?"

I am convinced that a love for God's word, a love that manifests itself in biblical meditation, can only be ignored by those in ministry leadership at great cost both to leader and follower alike. Why? Because effectiveness in ministry leadership is contingent upon an intellectual and experiential knowledge of who God is. And this knowledge is accurately informed by the revelation that God himself has provided in his word, the Bible.

My wife and I were engaged during a time prior to the days of cyberspace and e-mails and texting. Because we lived in different cities for most of our engagement, the vast majority of our communication consisted of handwritten letters, augmented by a weekly phone call and a voice recording on a cassette tape. Those letters written in my fiancée's handwriting became very precious to me. I *loved* those letters because they were sent to me from the one I loved; and through those letters I was not only made aware of events in her life, but I was given access into her heart. I would read and reread those letters, particularly the parts in which she spoke of her love for me and how much she longed for the time when we would be together again. This is how we should read Scripture. According to Soren Kierkegaard:

> To read the Bible as God's word, one must read it with his heart in his mouth, on tip-toe, with eager expectancy, in conversation with God. To read the Bible thoughtlessly or carelessly or academically or professionally is not to read the Bible as God's word. As one reads it as a love letter is read, then one reads it as the word of God.

The leader who practices biblical meditation makes the assumption that God has spoken and continues to speak today, and that he does so through Scripture. Any approach to leadership in ministry that does not embrace Scripture as being God's authoritative, inspired, and sufficient record of his truth, love, and holiness is not sustainable. How much does the word of God and your love for that word play directly into your leadership and ministry? How influential is the word of God in your development as a leader?

The Person Who Loves the Word Is One Who Will Memorize that Word

In Psalm 119:11 David gives this testimony: "I have stored up your word in my heart that I might not sin against you." In other words, David has so completely embraced the law that he cannot live beyond its bounds. Unlike David, many Christ followers today do not so love the word such that it becomes integrated with their personal holiness.

Let us return to Psalm 1:3. The operative phrase here tells us that "in his law he meditates day and night." This is not a call for believers to carry around scrolls of the Torah. Rather, it is a call to commit the law to memory, so that at any time, in any location, the believer can access Scripture, the word of God.

Why do so few of us engage in this vital exercise? I can think of very few reasons, really. First, we are not convinced it is really that important to do. Second, we are convinced we cannot do it due to time constraints or personal inabilities, imagined or real. Third, we have somehow been inoculated by past Scripture memory methods. Many of us received this inoculation as children while attending Sunday School. Those classes typically require students to learn a memory verse each week. Although a given verse ties into a given lesson, the range of verses to be memorized represents a scattered selection from various portions of the Bible. I still remember the verses I learned in Sunday School, such as Isaiah 53:6 and 1 John 1:9, which I memorized at age twelve. Make no mistake, I am grateful for the teachers who encouraged me to do so. But memorizing a verse from Isaiah one week and 1 John the next is similar to memorizing a bar or two of music from Mozart and then one or two from Beethoven.

I do not mean to diminish the good works that go on in our Sunday Schools, but I am soundly convinced that a person can memorize the thirty verses of Philippians chapter one much more quickly, and retain it much longer, than if that same person attempted to memorize thirty individual verses from various parts of the Bible. The simple reason is that the flow between sentences in a paragraph aids retention. By contrast, distinct and unrelated verses are more difficult for the human mind to assemble. Am I suggesting that there is no benefit to be gained from memorizing individual verses? Not at all. But our appreciation for those distinct verses is inevitably enhanced when we memorize the entire paragraph or chapter in which it is found.

I am reminded of a conversation I had with a good friend of mine, Bruce, who at the time was studying in our seminary. I was describing how a mutual friend of ours had encouraged me to take on the challenge of memorizing not just a few biblical verses here and there, but entire books of the Bible. Despite my enthusiasm over the personal discovery that this was actually within the realm of possibility for me, Bruce shared his own personal frustration. "I've tried and tried and just can't do it. Do you realize how embarrassing it is for me as a pastor not to be able to recite Scripture?" I asked him if he had any diagnosed learning disabilities. No, none. There was no question with respect to his earnest desire, yet somehow he was convinced that committing large portions of Scripture to memory was beyond his reach. I invited him to a challenge, convinced that we could learn a whole chapter together by the end of the school year. With no small degree of doubt he agreed.

I recommended we begin this effort by memorizing a single chapter before we took on the challenge of an entire book. Bruce thought this was a good idea, and we decided upon Romans 8, a rich passage with so many marvelous truths. Over the next few months we met weekly, adding four verses each time to our memory bank. I will never forget the smile and delight on Bruce's face when he recited all thirty-nine verses, word perfect! It wasn't just that we loved the hard work of memorizing Scripture; it was that we both loved Scripture and were committed to making it accessible to our hearts and minds whether we had a Bible handy or not. So what made the difference for Bruce? It was the same strategy that made a difference in my own journey, and can best be summarized in the following seven suggestions.

First of all, prayerfully seek a companion. Memorizing large portions of Scripture is seldom successful as a solo flight. A steady companion has proven to be the essential ingredient of success for many folks who attempt this important and difficult task. Although face-to-face meetings are ideal, they are not necessary. Over the past five years I have been working with my memory partner, Tim, on two major projects (Revelation and the Gospel of Mark). We have only met in person once. Knowing that every week I will be on the phone with my Scripture memory companion, who will be expecting me to have kept up with our memory target together, is very effective and positive peer pressure!

During my years as an undergrad, I decided to commit myself to a regimen of physical training. I wanted to get in as good physical shape as possible. This regimen included running a mile five times a week and a weight training program three times a week. After several frustrating, short-lived solo attempts at maintaining consistency, I commiserated with a friend in the dorm who, as it just so happened, was also failing to consistently keep to his exercise plan. We decided to coordinate our workout schedules, and we committed ourselves to three weekly workouts together. The change was remarkable. Invariably on the nights when I found ample excuses to miss a workout, Keith would be at my door, refusing to leave until I got into my sweats and joined him in the weight room.

Taking on the even more important challenge of memorizing Scripture entails very similar challenges. For the vast majority of us, the conviction that a particular exercise or discipline is very important, indeed essential, is inadequate for maintaining the discipline. I am soundly convinced of the importance and benefits of committing Scripture to memory, just as I was convinced of the importance and benefits of working out in the gym. But in both endeavors I maintained consistency only in partnership with another comrade on the journey. Prayerfully seek out a companion who is equally convinced of the necessity of this discipline.

Second, find a version of the Bible with which you are comfortable. Some translations are easier to memorize than others, and the version that best suits you often depends on your personal preferences. Regardless, memorize a version that you will most often use. This may call for a certain degree of experimentation, of trial and error, and may take some time. However, this is time well spent.

I had the thrill of encouraging a student of mine to join me in a Scripture memory project. However, this student discovered that the version I preferred to memorize was cumbersome for him. Likewise, I found his preferred version challenging in that it felt almost too conversational for me. Ultimately, we chose two different versions but continued to meet regularly knowing there was no *best* version to memorize. We all memorize differently. Memorizing Scripture is challenging enough on its own merit. There is no need to compound the challenge by plodding through a version that discourages rather than enhances the desire to carry on. Find a version of Scripture that facilitates memorizing for you personally.

Third, agree upon a reasonable length of weekly portion. There is no optimum amount of text that will suit each person, but the amount should be challenging enough to require consistent discipline. This may require you to willingly experiment, because the length of a given passage should be long enough to be challenging, yet not so long that you will get discouraged through a series of failed attempts. I am convinced that most of us can memorize more than we think we can. It simply may require that you unlearn some previously ineffective methods, and discover your own sweet spot, as it were.

My memory companion and I have landed upon four verses per week, or approximately one additional verse every other day. As we were discussing this, Tim, who is a good, hardworking Mennonite, could easily have found this effort to be, in his own words, paltry. But he agreed to this paltry effort because he, like me, understands that the issue here is sustainability, that is, maintaining for the long haul. In one of our e-mail exchanges he put it this way, "I was able to learn ten verses a week but completely unable to sustain ten verses a week." This work is not a race either against time or ourselves. The goal is not to memorize as much as we can, as quickly as we can. Rather the goal is to retain as much as we can for as long as we can. That is much more likely to happen through consistent, manageable, sustainable mouthfuls.

Fourth, commit yourself as much as possible to a weekly regular meeting. Leaving two weeks or more in between get-togethers, barring mitigating circumstances or holidays, will tend to undermine success. My weekly meeting with Tim over the phone is written in my calendar. When invitations to other meetings at the same time come in, I am simply able to say, "Sorry, I already have a commitment at that time. What other times fit your schedule?" By committing these meetings with Tim to my calendar I am reminding myself that this is a pivotal part of my week. Furthermore, the knowledge that my brother in Christ is carving out time in his busy schedule to hide the word in his heart, and is expecting me to do the same, has a way of encouraging me to maintain this rhythm. I find it interesting, if not sad, that we will carve out time for a weekly television program, refusing to miss it, barring a death in the family, yet find ample excuse for not investing the same level of commitment to a companionship that will put the truth and power of God's word in our hearts!

Fifth, don't allow the occasional spell of discouragement to dominate. There will be times when, for whatever reason, a passage just fails to "stick." There will be times when, after a few weeks without going over memorized material, you will think you lost it forever. However, experience has taught me that after two or three rehearsals, it all comes back. Overcoming discouragement requires, at times, a military mindset. An illustration may help clarify what I mean.

I attended Bible college in the United States when the Vietnam War was at its height. One of my classmates, John, who had already done his two year tour of duty prior to entering Bible college, told me about a discipline exercise he engaged in regularly during his training as a United States Marine. The exercise, which he usually did during his free time, involved dismantling his M16 rifle and reassembling it as quickly as he could, preferably within ninety seconds or less—blindfolded! Many of John's exercises in Vietnam were conducted at night. His rifle was not only his primary means of attack, it was also his primary defense mechanism.

While serving in the Marines, John had no problem choosing not to participate in certain completely legitimate activities, so that he could sit on the ground somewhere, blindfolded, and take his rifle apart and put it back together as quickly as possible. A single session could last for an hour or more. Why? He was convinced of two critical realities: first, he was involved in very real warfare, and second, his life very likely would depend on an intimate working knowledge of his weapon. He had to know his weapon so well that in the event of a jam or misfire he could remedy the situation as quickly as possible. More properly, he rightly believed that his very life depended on him knowing his weapon so well that he could operate it and, if need be, dismantle and reassemble it, even in the dark.

John was also convinced that even upon his return home from Vietnam, he would be engaged in a war that had far higher consequences at stake. He believed that the knowledge of his M16 rifle, which was essential to his survival in the theater of war, paled in comparison to the significance to his knowledge of the sword of the Spirit, the Bible.[18]

Paul's admonition to young Timothy was this: "Do your best to present yourself to God as one approved, a worker who has no need to be ashamed rightly handling the word of truth."[19] These are not unrelated directives. Serving as one who is approved unto God entails being one who has no need to be ashamed, and one who is unashamed is one who knows how to handle the word of truth correctly. I often wonder what it would be like if every ministry leader took the word of God as seriously as my friend John took his M16. In essence, John "memorized" his rifle not to impress his fellow soldiers but to better his chance of survival![20] Memorizing Scripture is hard work. You may experience a season of discouragement when it seems that you just cannot retain and recall the passage you have been working on. Persist. Dedicate yourself to the same depth of conviction and commitment as if you are a Marine whose life depends upon memorizing his weapon.

Sixth, review—DAILY if at all possible. Build Scripture memory review into your nighttime and morning rituals. In addition to regular devotional times that you may set aside, one of the wonderful aspects of this discipline is that it can be engaged in a number of contexts, almost any time. For example, you can rehearse a memorized passage when you are travelling in the car or on public transit, while taking a shower, exercising, folding laundry, mowing the lawn, or shoveling snow. A time I have found particularly helpful is while falling asleep at night. I find that intentionally occupying

18. Eph 6:16.

19. 2 Tim 2:15.

20. If Satan, the enemy, can downgrade the absolute necessity of the Word in our minds to the point that the Word has become more like a hobby, something we occasionally dabble in, then he has accomplished a major coup.

my mind with Scripture at the end of a challenging or busy day crowds out issues that might otherwise intrude on necessary rest. That is, my mind is occupied with *truth*, and not with the "what ifs" and "if onlys" of my imagination.

There is great benefit from augmenting the daily routine of Scripture memory with less frequent but extended rehearsals of longer passages. I have found that this kind of rhythm is difficult to sustain. Like a dedicated marathon runner, training for hours once a week is far less effective than training for shorter intervals on a daily basis.

Last, allow yourself reasonable flexibility. It is important to remind ourselves we are not sinning if we fail to keep up pace. Life brings its unexpected circumstances and opportunities, which, as James reminds us, are to be welcomed as friends, not intruders.[21] The challenge we often encounter involves maintaining the balance between viewing Scripture memory as requirement (something we *have* to do or *should* do) and a gift (something we *get* to do).

And the Benefit?

I have already suggested that Christ followers don't engage in the discipline of Scripture memory because they are not entirely convinced of its vital importance. Even the military motif of getting to know our weapon fails to move many of us because we are not aware of the outright frontal attacks that the enemy makes on a daily basis. Life is good! God seems to be blessing! When life is good, that sense of urgency is muted. Likewise, if the vast majority of our time is spent within the community of faith with other Christ followers, then the felt need to rightly handle the word of God becomes less pressing.

In the process of vetting some of this material for this book, my friend Tim asked me a very pointed and poignant question: "How has the essence of your love for Scripture changed since you started memorizing? Yes, you have more of it in your heart, but has it changed your delight in any measurable way?"

Great question, is it not?

Without question, my delight in the word has changed since I began memorizing major portions of Scripture. For me, this delight comes in

21. Jas 1:2, J. B. Phillips New Testament.

seeing that the word of God is indeed sharp and powerful,[22] capable of affecting substantial changes in my heart and mind. The challenge, it seems to me, is in quantifying those changes in "any measurable way." As Dallas Willard has said:

> Memorization of Scripture is one way of "taking charge" of the contents of our conscious thoughts, and of the feelings, beliefs and actions that depend on them . . . Our life takes on godly and good direction when our mind is consciously occupied with God's written words. Those words then increasingly eliminate the conscious mental contents that would surely lead us away from God.[23]

Indeed, for me the delight also comes in finding that I am not only capable of reciting Scripture, but that I am *thinking* it. The word gradually and continually becomes more and more woven into the tapestry of my thought life, which ultimately works its way into my speech. Again, drawing on the wisdom of Dallas Willard: "Through memorization God's words reside in our body, in our social environment, in the constant orientation of our will and in the depths of our soul They become a power, a substance, that sustains and directs us without our even thinking of them, and they emerge into conscious thought and action as needed."[24] Memorizing Scripture, then, enhances our knowledge of God, our worship of him, and our service to him. Yet despite the benefits I have mentioned, and many more besides, there is a potential downside that we must consider.

A Necessary Warning

The prophet Jeremiah reminds that "The heart is deceitful above all things, and desperately sick; who can understand it?"[25] The gratifying sense of accomplishment that one enjoys after committing significant portions of Scripture to memory can easily devolve into an unwholesome sense of pride. If this pride is allowed to take hold, then the benefit of memorizing Scripture is in danger of being undermined. Our gratitude needs to be based not upon what *we* have accomplished, but on the powerful effect that God can have on our life through his word.

22. Heb. 4:12.
23. Willard in Kang, *Scripture by Heart*, 8.
24. Ibid., 8.
25. Jer 17:9.

Satan is a master of spiritual martial arts. He often uses our own momentum to toss us beyond where we need or want to be. For instance, committing Scripture to memory out of a desire to follow David's example—hide the word in our hearts so that we might not sin against God—can easily push us into that sin of pride, just mentioned above. Consciously abandoning ourselves to the grace of God, of course, is essential to countering the enemy's attempts to derail us. Likewise, it is also essential that we intentionally pay attention to what the word is actually saying. In other words, reflect on, be attentive to, what you memorize.

The Person Who Loves the Word Is One Who Is Attentive to the Word

Unfortunately, we can easily allow our relationship to Scripture to devolve in the realm of pragmatism or utilitarianism. Our relationship with it can become what we *use* or merely what we *know* more than what we *love*. The person who loves the word is one who meditates on that word and one who memorizes that word. It is possible, however, for a person in ministry leadership to engage in Scripture meditation and memorization while allowing that word to have little or no impact on his or her heart, mind, soul, and strength.

Loving the Lord with all our heart, mind, soul, and strength is made manifest in our relationship with the word. Love for the word will be made manifest and will be enhanced by our commitment to meditate on Scripture; and our effectiveness in meditation will be nurtured by our commitment to memorize Scripture. But, ultimately, our love for the word begins with and is maintained by our choice to be attentive to God's revelation and Scripture. The choice to be attentive to Scripture is based upon the conviction that it is here where we find truth about who we are and how we fit into this magnificent universe. It is here where all ambiguity is removed with respect to the question of who God is and what God really expects from us.

There is no meter that can gauge the depth and authenticity of our love for the word. But a helpful, though not always pleasant, exercise is to reflect on this question: How does the amount of time we spend in meditating and memorizing God's precious word compare with the time we invest in other activities—including legitimate activities like social networking and recreation; and essential ministerial activities like planning and executing events and ministering to those we are privileged to lead? The more shallow and superficial our relationship with the word, the more poverty-stricken our ministry will be. That is absolutely guaranteed.

We must avoid two extremes when providing leadership ministry to local congregations. The first is getting bogged down in lecture-like attention to theological minutia and taking people deep into the mineshaft of intellectual engagement without coming back up into the fresh air of relevant personal application. Nuggets of gold are of no value when they stay deep in the mine. These nuggets must be brought out, refined, crafted, and processed in crucible of life application. The other extreme to be avoided is failure to push people beyond the ankle-deep waters of safe, superficial theological engagement. Without a push into the deep end, congregants cannot find answers to tough questions, or at least they do not necessarily come quickly or easily to them. Maintaining a balance between these two contrasting tendencies is challenging to say the least, but it behooves us as leaders to demonstrate the fact that love for the Lord calls for an organic connection between heart and mind. Both our heart and mind need the nourishment that Scripture alone can provide.

Few would deny the disconcerting decline in biblical literacy that seems to be sweeping through many portions of the church in pandemic proportions. I have yet to come across anyone in church leadership who is happy or content with where their congregations are in terms of Bible knowledge or awareness. As Robert Dunham has discovered, "They want to learn, to explore the faith at a deeper level, *and they want that depth to be part of what they hear from the pulpit.*"[26]

One of the ways ministry leaders can increase the level of biblical literacy in a congregation is *not* to dumb down what is taught from church pulpits or studied in small groups. It is essential that leaders have an accurate awareness of their congregants' Bible knowledge and growth trajectory. Equally important, however, is that leaders are cognizant of where people should be. The writer to the Hebrews was aware of, and deeply concerned about, the condition of his readers in relation to the word.

> For by this time you ought to be teachers, you need someone to teach you again the basic principles of the oracles of God. You need milk, not solid food, for everyone who lives on milk is unskilled in the word of righteousness, since he is a child. But solid

26. Dunham, "Loving God," 21 (emphasis added).

food is for the mature, for those who have their powers of discernment trained by constant practice to distinguish good from evil.[27]

Statements such as this, of course, imply that the writer, without boasting, was able to digest the "solid food" of the word. Why should we expect any less of our leaders in ministry today?

So Now What?

Should we be tempted to consider that the word of God is less than essential or even unworthy of our love, we need only to remind ourselves of the words of David: "I bow down toward your holy temple and give thanks to your name for your steadfast love and your faithfulness, for *you have exalted above all things your name and your word*."[28] In David's time, the phrase "name of God" was typically used in reference to the essence or character of God himself. God himself used the term in his response to Solomon's prayer of dedication for the temple when he said, "I have heard your prayer and your plea, which you have made before me. I have consecrated this house that you have built, by putting my name there forever. My eyes and my heart will be there forever."[29] David postures the word of God as something that, along with the name of God, has been exalted by God above all else. In light of this it is difficult to imagine loving God with all we are in the absence of a love for his word.

The word of God is not a reference text that we consult every now and then. It must play a pivotal role in everything we do and are as the church. Our worship of God is to be guided by the word; our discipleship ministries are to be rooted in the word; our service to the world around us is to be inspired by and consistent with the word. That being the case, those of us who serve as leaders in the church and world must be committed lovers of the word. Does this imply that all elders or deacons, for instance, should have the equivalent of a Seminary-level grasp of Scripture? Of course not! But, if a person is not regularly taking time to nourish his or her own soul on Scripture, if Scripture is not becoming more and more a part of a person's spiritual DNA, in other words, if that person does not love the word, then

27. Heb 5:12–14.

28. Ps 138:2, italics added.

29. 1 Kgs 9:3.

why on Earth would we consider him or her fit to shepherd the people of God?

In a speech given at the 1974 International Congress of World Evangelism in Lausanne, Switzerland, Francis Schaeffer said, "Holding to a strong view of Scripture or not holding to it is the watershed of the evangelical world."[30] One has to wonder how many people within Evangelicalism would agree with Dr. Schaeffer's statement now, four decades later! Dr. Schaeffer's brand of loyalty to Scripture is most clearly demonstrated on the local level only when we, as leaders in ministry, are consistently growing in our love for the word.[31]

As we immerse ourselves in memorizing and meditating upon the word of God, and grow in our love for it, we will soon discover with all clarity what God loves and, therefore, what he expects us in turn to love. The next chapter takes us into a consideration of a second vital object of our love, namely, the church.

For Group Discussion:

1. As a group, discuss your response to the question that Bill uses in his Homiletics class, that is, "Do you consider Scripture more an authority or a gift/treasure?"

2. Likewise discuss the second question, "What difference would it make?"

For Personal Reflection:

1. Prayerfully take inventory of how you generally spend the hours on an average day. Identify one activity that, though perhaps not sinful, is robbing you of potential time to be attentive to God through Scripture. What would help you retrieve that time? Don't try to initially carve out an hour or more right away. Begin small and gradually crowd out the less productive activities with Scripture meditation and memorization.

30. Schaeffer, *No Final Conflict*, 48.

31. There is, of course, a place for public and corporate affirmation of what Schaeffer calls a "strong view of Scripture" in the classroom, around the debate table, and in denominational statements of faith.

2. Reflect personally on the questions the author asked at the end of the section on meditation: "How much does the word of God and your love for that word play directly into your leadership and ministry? How influential is the word of God in your development as a leader?"

Prayer: *Gracious Father, next to the unspeakable gift of your Son the Lord Jesus and the sweet presence of your Holy Spirit, the greatest gift you have given us is your word. I am so thankful. Please create in my heart a love and longing for your word that is homesick when absent from it. Generate the desire and the discipline to meditate on your word daily and to memorize it so that all I am and do, think and say, may make you large. I ask this by your grace and for your glory, in Jesus' wonderful name. Amen.*

THREE

Love for the Church

THE CHURCH HAS ALWAYS been a part of my life. Born to missionary parents in Chad, Africa, and raised in a parsonage in Toronto, Canada, my whole life has been profoundly impacted by my relation with the church. I have lived and ministered long enough to witness a wide array of internal changes in the church: the good, the bad, and the ugly. As well, I have observed shifts in external attitudes toward the church. Indeed, the church has lost ground in terms of its popularity and influence at all levels in our society. The global role of the church has waned significantly. Few would argue against this observation. In the early twentieth century, Karl Barth identified the multiplicity of churches as one of the most powerful factors in alienating people from the church.[1] More recently, Kevin DeYoung and Ted Kluck[2] suggest at least four reasons for this. First, they cite *missiological* reasons: church leaders are failing to retain younger generations and seem to be ignoring key societal issues. Second, they cite the *personal* reasons: from the perspective of those outside the church it appears that we are anti-women, anti-gay, judgmental, and closed-minded. By contrast, church insiders, that is, regular-to-occasional attenders, have felt wounded, stifled, and perhaps even deceived by church leadership. Furthermore, many of these insiders consider our Sunday gatherings to be a drag. Third, DeYoung and Kluck cite *historical* reasons: the church has some unfortunate baggage from Constantine's introduction of Christianity as the state religion, to the Spanish Inquisition to the Crusades, and even to the church's capitulation to the Third Reich in World War II.[3] And fourth, and I would suggest the

1. Barth, *The Church and the Churches*, 9.
2. DeYoung and Kluck, *Why We Love the Church*, 16–18.
3. For an excellent, eye-opening work on this sensitive issue see Jantzen, *Faith and*

most disconcerting, they cite *theological* reasons: We have shown ourselves incapable of isolating or identifying a universally agreed upon concept or definition of what the church, in fact, is. For many people, this theological muddle amounts to little more than the plurality of Christianity! To this way of thinking, wherever there are two or three Christians who love Jesus, and who love each other, there is a church! Put another way, the introduction of man-made structures and institutional apparatuses can move us further away from Jesus' kingdom agenda.

For too many people the church represents the source of some of their life's greatest disappointments, wounds, or scars. For these people, the thought of loving the church may present an enormous challenge. In reality, however, these people have not been disappointed with or wounded by the true church of Christ; rather they have been harmed by people who may not actually be a part of Christ's body. I am not denying for a moment that some professed Christians live in ways that are profoundly contrary to the character of Christ. Indeed, there has been far too much carnage left in the wake of too many Christians who, through a misguided sense of leadership or authority or through a blatant disregard for life principles exemplified and commanded by Christ, have wounded those to whom they are responsible.

People's disappointment or anger with the church, then, has more to do with human failings. When individual church leaders insist on living or serving independently from the indwelling Christ, and refuse to live under his lordship, then is it any wonder people fall out of love with the church? This raises an important question: What precisely is the church? When I talk about the church, I refer to Christians in relationship both with Christ, the head of the Church, and with each other; the way Christ intended. I am talking about the bride of Christ that he loves and gave himself for that he might present it to himself, a glorious church without any spot or wrinkle or any such thing.[4] I am talking about the reality of community without which I cannot grow as one indwelt by the living Christ.

We are not called to love a concept, an organization or institution, a tradition or denomination. We are called to love each other, forgiven people who share a common life, the life of Christ, and a common loyalty to the *missio dei*, the mission of God in this needy world. The difficulty, of course, is that the ideal is so often blurred by present realities that include

---

Fatherland.

4. Eph. 5:25–27.

disobedient Christ followers as well as a world antagonistic to Christ and his wonderful, redemptive purposes.

The approach of this chapter, therefore, is not to turn a magnifying glass on all the foibles and failures of the church down through the centuries. Nor is it my purpose here to roll out a litany of statistics that manifest a disconcerting hemorrhaging in church attendance. There is nothing redemptive or helpful to be gained in doing so. Rather, our efforts here will be poured into underscoring the nature and the mission of the church, and reminding ourselves of how deeply Christ loves his church.

Regarding our love for the church, I suggest that our love needs to be undergirded by two foundations: a biblical understanding of the nature and mission of the church and an appreciation for the depth of Christ's love for the church. I am not attempting to duplicate any of the numerous excellent theological works that pay careful and detailed attention to the nature and mission of the church.[5] Rather, by presenting a distilled version of these truths, it is my hope that we will grow deeper in our love for the church.

Biblical Understanding of the Nature of the Church

In a manner somewhat reminiscent of my own country's felt need to redefine family, it seems that, whether intentionally or inadvertently, we have developed a need to redefine church. For this reason, I can no longer assume that all readers understand what I mean when I suggest that love for the church is essential for effective leadership in ministry. Exactly what church are we to love? Such confusion is not a recent development. In his address to the global Second Word Conference on Faith and Order in 1937, Karl Barth stated:

> But where, who, and what is the Church? What a dissipation of the spiritual and material energies of the mission work arises from the fact that there is not one Church but many, and what a hindrance to the hearing of its message, what a bewilderment to its less attentive hearers, what a burden to the more serious, is the fact that these churches are in manifold conflict with each other.[6]

5. A mere sampling would include Erickson's *Christian Theology*, Oden's *Life in the Spirit: Systematic Theology: Volume Three*, Grudem's *Systematic Theology*, and Grenz's *Theology for the Community of God*.

6. Barth, *The Church and the Churches*, 5.

Taking a cue from Barth, we must delineate the essence of the church before we can address the critical issue of our love for the church. Put another way, what elements or dynamics must be present in order for the church to exist?

I am one who believes that two or three people sipping cappuccinos and talking about spiritual issues in Starbucks are *not*, in essence, what the church *is*. I thoroughly enjoy such activities, and such activities may be an example of what the church *does* from time to time, but I believe casual engagement with spiritual issues falls short of biblical precedent and principle in terms of what the church *is*. Let us pause for a moment to consider Jesus' statement in Matthew 18:20: "For where two or three are gathered in my name, there am I among them." Jesus did not say two or three people gathered in his name constitute a church. In this text he simply promised he would be among them. As meaningful and significant as a spiritual discussion in Starbucks may be, the absence of certain elements preclude this casual meeting from being a church. Does the church benefit from or need such encounters? Of course. But there is more.

Essential Ecclesiology

If, as the Nicene Creed reminds us, there is one holy catholic apostolic church, why is there still so much confusion and division with respect to the meaning of the word "church"; and why is there such a vast array of convictions relative to the reason for the church's existence? Despite the fact that the church was birthed over two millennia ago, and today exists literally around the globe, there is still a multitude of often contradictory assertions (and no universally accepted definition) of what constitutes the church. I have to wonder if this persistent ambiguity is not rooted in the fact that the church exists both in theory and in praxis, in doctrine or theology; and in the concrete, incarnational reality here on Earth. Often, and unfortunately, the two are blurred. Add to this the fairly recent proliferation of ecclesial paradigms. New models of how to do or be the church have appeared almost with rhythmic regularity over the past several decades. As a result we are not as free to use the same monikers as we did previously. For example, terms such as Evangelical, Mainline, Neo-Orthodox, and Liberal do not enjoy the same currency as in the past. Consider, for instance, a few of the many labels that have been added or resurrected recently that now come under the rubric of Evangelical: seeker friendly/sensitive; liturgical;

charismatic; blended worship; megachurch; house church, emergent, missional, and even "hipster" church.[7] If this plethora of ecclesial expressions were not enough of a challenge, what does one do with the ever-increasing presence of cyber-churches that are readily available on the Internet? Ultimately, let us remember that the presence of numerous expressions of the church does not have to undermine the conviction that there remains one holy, apostolic, universal (catholic) church.

Beyond the proliferation of labels, if you were to ask any number of church attenders or persons on the street what comes to mind when they think about "church," more than likely you will get a wide variety of responses. Some people will think immediately of a building at a specific location. Others will describe a gathering that takes place during the weekend in which a pastor or priest speaks, people sing, possibly sacraments are observed, and people leave. Others may think on the macro scale of the universal church that consists of all blood-bought Christ followers.

But the confusion does not stop here. It is difficult to deny many of the indictments brought against the church down through the years. These accusations, however sensational, tend to focus on one or more of the layers of institutionalization, or on unfortunate errors and misjudgments of officials, or on theory and debate that have built up a lava-like crust. Regardless, the essence of the church is buried. Thomas Oden says it eloquently:

> When administration is reduced to management, evangelism to technique, soul care to therapeutic strategy, and preaching to rhetoric, the doctrine of the church has been misplaced.[8]

Surely there must be some identifiable hallmarks, some predicates that allow us to identify the genuine church. Two sixteenth-century reformers, Martin Luther and John Calvin, shared a similar conviction in this regard. Luther's conviction is summarized in what has come to be known as the Augsburg Confession of 1530. In it, Luther describes the church as "the congregation of saints in which the gospel is rightly taught and the Sacraments rightly administered" (Article 7).[9] The challenge before us, then, is to crack through the layers of theory, history, and circumstance that too often have been identified inaccurately as synonymous with the church itself, and

7. See McCracken, *Hipster Christianity*.

8. Oden, *Life in the Spirit*, 265.

9. Cited in Grudem, *Systematic Theology*, 865.

in so doing expose from Scripture what constitutes the one, holy, catholic (universal), apostolic church, the church we are to love.

A Gathered Community

Western culture functions largely under the domineering influence of individualism. So pervasive has been its impact that the autonomy of the individual has set the cadence and tone of our theological reflections. Church has become a place where many people go to receive help and encouragement in order to live out a Christian life—individually. In my mind the tyranny of individualism within the church is a challenge that parallels any external opposition. It is at the root of attitudes of entitlement and consumerism that we, as leaders, are so quick to decry.

Interestingly enough, there are indications that more and more people are calling into question the individualism of the Enlightenment. These people recognize how germane and essential community is to our humanness. Likewise, Western theologians are affirming the need to rediscover the communal nature of what it means to be the church. Kevin Giles, for instance, states the following:

> To suggest that the Bible is ultimately about individual salvation, or that the church is but a local assembly of individuals who are bound together only by their personal associations, or that each individual congregation is in no profound way linked with other congregations, introduces ideas alien to biblical thinking. Those who suggest such things reflect their own cultural values, not the values of the biblical writers.[10]

It is important to clarify what Scripture means by the term "church," as translated into our English word. "It is from Jesus' own carefully and accurately remembered personal phrase, 'my church'—spoken first in Aramaic and later in Greek—that the Greek term *ekklesia* came to have preeminence thereafter over all other terms used to describe the community of faith."[11] "My church" is a compound term rooted in two Greek words, *ek* (out or from) and the verb *kaleo* (to call, or name). Scriptural writers used this word to refer to the act of gathering people who were called by God for the purpose of hearing the apostles teaching, the gospel, or fellow-

10. Giles, *What on Earth Is the Church?* 21.

11. Oden, *Systematic Theology*, 266.

shipping at the table.[12] But this word was also used to designate gatherings of unbelievers who were not a part of the church.[13] The emphasis was on "gathering" and not on "called out" or "separate," whether in reference to the legislative assembly in Rome or a gathering of Christians. Thus, the early usage of the word did not apply to the group after the assembly had dispersed. However, over time the use and meaning of the word morphed until it referred not just to the act of assembling but to those assembled.

God looked upon his people in ancient Israel in a way that is similar to *ekklesia*. The Old Testament provides a number of examples. The Lord directed Moses to "Gather the people to me, that I may let them hear my words, so that they may learn to fear me all the days that they live on the earth, and that they may teach their children so."[14] In the Greek translation of the Hebrew Scriptures[15] we find the word "gather" (Hebrew *qahal*) translated by a word sharing the same root as the word *ekklesia*. The apostle Stephen, using the Greek word *ekklesia*, referred to Israel as the *assembly* in the wilderness.[16] Does this mean that ancient Israel and the church are one and the same? I am not convinced. Rather, as Wayne Grudem has stated, "The New Testament church is an assembly of God's people that simply continues in the pattern of assemblies of God's people found throughout the Old Testament."[17] What we can draw from this brief consideration is this: the emphasis of the word *ekklesia* that we have translated into the term "church" is the communal, gathering dimension of what it means to be the church. Individuals who isolate themselves from gathering with other Christ followers, therefore, cannot be said to be acting like or reflecting the nature of the church.

Christocentric and Trinity-Based

The church we are to love is not only to be a gathered community; it is to be Christocentric, that is, centered on Christ himself. It is easy for us to get swept up in causes that stir our hearts, and in the process direct our focus past Christ. It is in and through Christ that the kingdom of God is being

12. Ibid., 265.

13. Acts 19:32, 39, 41.

14. Deut 4:10.

15. This is known as the Septuagint.

16. Acts 7:38.

17. Grudem, *Systematic Theology*, n. 2, 854.

established on Earth. Under the Mosaic covenant of the Old Testament, the kingdom of God, that is his reign, was expressed in and through his chosen, faithful people of Israel. That same kingdom rule of God, through the establishment of the new covenant, is now being manifest in and through the church. The church is God's chosen community through which the kingdom of God is to be extended and established in this world. Gordon Smith emphasizes this fact: "To live in the kingdom of God is to come under the salvation and authority of Jesus of Nazareth."[18] Jesus himself identified Peter's confession, in which he professed Jesus to be the messiah, as the rock upon which he would build his church.[19] The apostle Paul reiterated this truth when he reminded his Corinthian readers that no other foundation exists for the church than Christ himself.[20] "Whether Christ is or is not present is the question of whether the church exists or does not exist."[21]

Jesus' proclamation that he would build his church[22] with such effect that the gates of hades will be unable to resist is often taken to be the definitive statement of the fact that the church is primarily and fundamentally the work of Christ. But, as Thomas Oden reminds us, the church is the handiwork of all three members of the godhead in the respect that, "the One whose electing love calls the living community one by one into being is the Father. The One embodied in the church is the Son as head of the body; the One who brings together the community of life in the spirit is God the Spirit."[23]

The church is also Christocentric in the sense that it is *his* church. Jesus affirmed this without hesitation or apology in Matthew 16:18 when he declared "I will build *my* church and the gates of hell shall not prevail against it." We would do well to remember this, and then remind each other when issues of entitlement or even strategic planning arise. It is not *our* church; never has been, never will be. The fact that Jesus made this statement toward the end of his earthly ministry reminds us not only that the church is ultimately Christ's personal possession but that it is his own handiwork—a work that continues even in his bodily absence from this world. In truth, the church is not the result of human initiative or common

18. Smith, *Essential Spirituality*, 63.

19. Matt 16:18.

20. 1 Cor 3:11.

21. Oden, *Life in the Spirit*, 298.

22. Matt 16:18.

23. Oden, *Life in the Spirit*, 261.

interest. Rather, it is Christ who is responsible for building his church and we, as members of Christ's body, are but called by the Father and united by the Spirit. Therefore we can take no pride in any "successes" the Lord may allow. Everything Christ elects to do through us as his church is strictly by his grace and for his glory! Luke reminds us of this reality when he tells us, "And the Lord added to their number day by day those who were being saved."[24] No human can claim ownership of the church. "The church exists because God wills it to be so, not because persons first contractually or voluntarily agree that they desire to become a redemptive community."[25]

Because, as we have seen, the church is God's idea, called out by the Father, being built by Christ and sustained by the Holy Spirit, our love for the church cannot be directed toward anything that is the result of our efforts to organize or design. We are to love God's own precious, blood-bought possession, his bride. The problem, unfortunately, is that all too often our efforts, our planning and activities (or lack thereof), demand our attention and eclipse the wonder of what the living Christ desires to do among his people. If we can explain the impact that our presence has on the church (by anything other than the supernatural working of the living Christ through the power and presence of the Holy Spirit), then we must honestly recognize who is doing the building, for what purpose, and for whose glory.

Multi-Directional in Emphasis

Soren Kierkegaard once stated, "Life is lived forwards but understood backwards."[26] A thoughtful glance backwards into the history of the early church is preserved for us in the book of Acts. This book sheds some light on those elements that are essential to the existence of the church. The purpose of revisiting the New Testament church is not to tease out direct, specific ways and means for expressing the church in our day. Simply, we in the West or Global North do not live in a first-century Middle-Eastern context. Likewise, we should not succumb to the tendency to romanticize the early church. We often think of it in glowing terms but fail to recall the divisive issues, heresies, even instances of moral failure and hypocrisy that they experienced. Having said that, however, Scripture provides us with

24. Acts 2:47.
25. Oden, *Systematic Theology*, 270.
26. Cited in Viola and Barna, *Pagan Christianity?* xiii.

some important insights: "The practices of the first-century church were the natural and spontaneous expression of the divine life that indwelt the early Christians . . . The first-century church teaches us how the life of God is expressed when a group of people begin to live by it together."[27]

Acts 2:42 describes the church as being dedicated to apostolic teaching, to community, to breaking of bread (sacrament), and to corporate worship. Three directional emphases or themes, if you will, are evident in Luke's account in Acts: *upward* (the worship of God), *inward* (community/fellowship and the building up of the body of Christ), and *outward* (service and evangelism).

All three must be present because all are of equal significance in discerning the essential nature and mission of the church. Focus on one theme to the neglect of the others inevitably diminishes the vitality and effectiveness of the church. One has to wonder if such imbalances are not at the root of the disillusionment that many have experienced in their relation to the church. For example, a church that overemphasizes the sacramental dimension of worship and teaching (upward and/or inward) may generate concern over the lack of service ministries and intentional efforts to introduce people to Christ through conversion. By the same token, a church that overemphasizes outreach and evangelism (outward) may leave its members longing for the intimate experience of God through sacrament and the Word (upward). Historically, the unity of the body of Christ has been undermined by an overemphasis on one or even two themes to the neglect of the other. It is only when all three themes are woven into "a threefold chord that cannot be easily broken" that the essence of the church is understood, appreciated, and more importantly demonstrated.

Unapologetic about the Gospel

If the church is to reflect the life and ministry of Jesus, it must be rooted in the gospel. In one of his first recorded public teaching statements, Jesus declared that he had been anointed for the very purpose of preaching the gospel.[28] The first recorded words of Jesus in Mark's gospel are simply this: "The time is fulfilled, the kingdom of God is at hand; repent and believe in the gospel."[29] Some translations accurately use the phrase "good news"

27. Ibid., xix.
28. Luke 4:18–19.
29. Mark 1:15.

for gospel.[30] The church possesses and is possessed by the good news of the gospel, and the transmission of this good news has been entrusted to the church. The gospel reminds us of the reason for our existence (we are the church solely because of the good news), and the gospel represents the purpose of our mission. *Remove the gospel and we have no reason to explain why the church should be here.*

The significance of the church's actual mission has been noticeably undermined by the increasing influence of an individualistic mindset. This mindset interprets the gospel to be primarily good news on the personal, individual level. It is about *my* personal relationship with *my* Lord and Savior, Jesus Christ: "you in your small corner and I in mine." But good news that affects only the individual represents a truncated gospel. As Miroslav Volf said, "'Gospel' always involves a way of living in a given social environment as a Christian community."[31] The very nature of the gospel implies a corporate dimension; it assumes the church.

It is not the blatant denial or rejection of the gospel that is hurting the church today. A far more insidious harm comes when we gloss over or minimize the centrality of the cross. For some people this glossing over is borne from a genuine but misguided desire for a more palatable message that, unfortunately and inevitably, dulls the keenness of the gospel's sharp edge. Attempts to communicate a less-offensive gospel demand that we avoid Scripture passages that remind us of the highly offensive nature of the true gospel for some. Paul states clearly in 1 Corinthians 1:22–23 that "Jews demand signs and Greeks seek wisdom, but we preach Christ crucified, a stumbling block to Jews and folly to Gentiles, but to those who are called, both Jews and Greeks, Christ the power of God and the wisdom of God." There is a vast difference, however, between being offended by the cross of Christ and being offended by insensitive, arrogant Christians! Paul was not ashamed of this gospel because he was unshakably convinced that its power provides salvation to everyone who believes.[32] It is not our responsibility to help people get over the stumbling block of the cross. That responsibility falls to the ministry of the Holy Spirit, and he does a wonderful and far better job than we ever could! *Remove the cross and we have no reason for the good news of the gospel, in fact, we have* no *gospel.*

30. See NIV for instance.
31. Volf, *Captive to the Word*, 67.
32. Rom 1:16.

One of the most powerful expressions of this truth has affected me very personally and very deeply. I refer to a message by C. J. Mahaney in which he said the following:

> In his righteous judgment God has determined that the just penalty for sin is death and without the shedding of blood there is no remission of sin. Now sin has been committed by man and therefore only man can atone for that sin. But here's my dilemma, I can't atone for my sin. I can't! I cannot satisfy God's righteous requirement. My disobedience condemns me before a righteous God and I'm captive to sin. It is humanly impossible for me to free myself from sin. A divine rescue is necessary. I NEED A SAVIOR! I need a savior![33]

It is for this reason that we are called. It is for this reason we must never minimize, marginalize, or apologize for the gospel that is anchored in the cross and resurrection of Jesus. How can we *ever* get tired of hearing about, or get used to, what the cross means to us as the bride of Christ and, more importantly, what it meant to Jesus? Anytime coolness in my heart develops toward the cross I remind myself that *I need a savior*—not just for my sins of the past and my hope in the future, but for today, every day!

Although Scripture is abundantly clear with respect to the centrality of the gospel through the cross and resurrection of Christ, it is relatively silent on the matter of methodology, that is, *how* the good news is to be manifest within the body of Christ.[34] Using any number of creative methods, it is possible to convey the centrality of the gospel with no compromise. Unfortunately, as often as not, it is those at the point of methodology that discrepancies and dissension arise.

There is also a tendency in most of us to judge other expressions of the church or methodologies from the vantage point of our own personal history and theological preferences. We are prone to assess different expressions of the church from the comfort of our own niche.[35] Furthermore, our inclination toward one orientation over others commonly is reflective of our spiritual giftedness. People endowed with spiritual gifts of compassion and mercy, not surprisingly will exercise those gifts. These people will be dismayed when a church organization pours energy and funds into new

33. Mahaney, "Atonement." See online for a poignant portion of this message.

34. Attention will be given in the next chapter to the matter of conveying the good news with those outside the church.

35. Oden, *Life in the Spirit*, 262.

sound equipment, which are intended to enhance corporate worship at the expense of meeting the social needs that exist right on the doorstep of the church. It is tragic how often, both on the individual and corporate levels, we respond with egocentric fear toward expressions of the church that exist outside of our own traditions or personal experiences. I am not insinuating that all Christians should completely agree on every fine point of doctrine or polity. This is not possible or even necessary. Indeed, I am convinced that our shared love for the church is not contingent upon such uniformity or agreement. The concept of "loving my neighbor as myself" will be expressed first within the community of believers, whether or not we are in agreement on all issues. In fact, Jesus stressed the point that *this* is how the world will know we are his disciples: we may not agree on everything, but despite this by God's grace we are still able to love our brothers and sisters genuinely.

Some may find reason to be concerned over such a statement, fearing that it belies a willingness to capitulate in a way that will open the flood gates of compromise; that the standards or truth will, of necessity, need to be lowered. On the contrary; our wholehearted love for the Lord that manifests itself in our genuine love for the church should bolster our commitment to resist compromise on any biblical truth.

Reason for the Church's Existence

Why does the church exist? How does the church fit into God's overarching metanarrative, his story of redemption? How do we know if we are on course for fulfilling Christ's purpose for his church? Is numerical growth the most accurate indicator that a church is fulfilling its mandate in this world? Questions such as these are not merely theoretical. They have profound practical impact; for the moment we lose a sense of purpose or direction, our ability to lead and minister effectively is compromised. This holds true regardless of the capacity in which that leadership is exercised, be it vocational pastoral or lay-elder or deacon. Recognizing the danger of oversimplification, I am convinced that we could forego many hours of unnecessary discussion if we intentionally call to mind the reasons why we exist as the church.

When we allow a "bottom line" mentality to dominate the "how" and "why" of church leadership, ministry leaders are likely to find themselves in a precarious situation.[36] For example, if the attendance numbers shows a steady decline and the budget is not met, leaders will think that something, or more likely someone, needs to change. Too often decisions in the area of church leadership staffing resemble that of a major league sports team rather than a community that is created and lead by the Holy Spirit. If a sport team's win and loss ledger is tilted toward the "lose" column, who typically ends up being the casualty? As often as not it is the coach, not the board of governors or even the players on the field. In a similar way, I know of too many church scenarios where a numerical decline was rather hastily attributed to the leadership of the senior pastor.[37] I am not denying the impact of senior leadership on church growth and decline realities, nor do I deny the fact that some lead pastors have single-handedly lead their congregations into decline. My point is that the purpose of the church is not primarily to grow numerically. There are other dimensions of growth that cannot be displayed on spreadsheets and charts, and we need to be prepared for the fact that "The more strictly you adhere to the teachings of Jesus, the smaller the church will 'grow.'"[38]

I suggest it is not difficult to tease out a meaningful, uncomplicated summary of reasons for the church's existence in our world today. As a called out community, the church does not exist to cloister itself in isolation from the world. Rather it exists so that people can gather to celebrate God's grace and then return to the world as the conduit of that grace. I must agree with Karl Barth who saw the task of the church being the proclamation of the gospel in all its fullness, that is, in Christ Jesus "the sin of all men, their contradiction against God and their own inner self-contradiction is done to death, taken away, forgiven, and exists no more."[39] The church exists to exalt God and proclaim his redemptive purposes in Christ. Paul described his Corinthian readers as being an epistle read by all, "And you show that you are a letter from Christ delivered by us, written not with ink but with the Spirit of the living God, not on tablets of stone but on tablets of human hearts."[40] It is essential to note that Paul's reminder suggested a corporate,

36. This mentality reflects a North American corporate mindset that is not informed by biblical principle.

37. I recognize that a shift toward the term "lead pastor" from the former designation "senior pastor" has occurred in recent years. Because readers of this book will (hopefully) represent a range of generations, I am choosing to use these terms interchangeably.

38. Galli cited in Carlson and Lueken, *Renovation*, 104.

39. Barth, *The Church and the Churches*, 10.

40. 2 Cor 3:3.

concerted effort, and not a solo performance! It is one thing to be enabled and freed through knowing who we are in Christ as individuals, but unless we hold a high view of our *corporate* identity as the church, we will never participate in God's redemptive purposes for the church as he intended.

The *upward* purpose of the church is to worship God. Worship, in essence, is ascribing worth to that which is worshipped. How do we do this as a corporate body? It is not a complex matter. The apostle Peter clearly states, "As each has received a gift, use it to serve one another, as good stewards of God's varied grace: whoever speaks, as one who speaks oracles of God; whoever serves, as one who serves by the strength that God supplies—in order that in everything God may be glorified through Jesus Christ. To him belong glory and dominion forever and ever. Amen."[41] In other words, every ministry in the church, without exception, every demonstration of the Spirit's power through the gifts he bestows, must have as its fundamental upward purpose the glorification of Christ, that is, to make him large.

The *inward* purpose of the church is the building up of Christians. Our inward purpose is not to ensure that all our personal needs might be met and our wants satisfied. The New Testament church demonstrates that the advent of the Holy Spirit, as described in Acts 2, in no way dispenses with the need for qualified teachers. Thus, the suggestion that a person only needs the Holy Spirit and the Bible, and therefore has no need to be taught in the Scriptures through gifted individuals (that God has equipped and placed strategically within the local fellowship), is to misread or neglect altogether numerous passages of Scripture. The early Christians devoted themselves to sitting under the apostles' teaching. The apostle Paul reminds us that God has given the church the gift of "pastor/teachers,"[42]—people gifted and mandated with the responsibility of teaching the members of the body of Christ in a way that will move them toward being more like Christ. Jesus referred to the Holy Spirit as the Spirit of truth, and Jesus promised us that the Holy Spirit would guide us into all truth.[43] John Stott reasons that "wherever the Spirit of truth is at work, truth matters."[44] The church we are to love is the church dedicated to and guided by God's truth revealed through Scripture.

41. 1 Pet 4:10–11.
42. Eph 4:11–16.
43. John 16:13.
44. Stott, *The Living Church*, 23.

Teaching of this nature is contingent upon and concerned about truth. For early Christians this teaching was engaged in community. The early Christ followers devoted themselves to both the apostles' teaching and to fellowship.[45] This fellowship consisted of much more than sharing refreshments and conversation following a service. This fellowship entailed a sharing in common. Members of the early church expressed this fellowship through the distribution of possessions among those who had material needs. Theirs was a generous fellowship! Perhaps one of the most striking descriptions of the church in Luke's account in Acts is that "There was not a needy person among them, for as many as were owners of lands or houses sold them and brought the proceeds of what was sold and laid it at the apostles' feet, and it was distributed to each as any had need."[46] What an amazing testimony!

In the light of other Scripture passages, it is difficult to sustain the argument that the early Christians invested everything into a common pot and did not own any private property. As John Stott has said, "The prohibition of private property is a Marxist, not a Christian doctrine."[47] Those blessed with material possessions maintained a loose grip on them, making them readily available to those in need. It seems that such a church, one that is committed to the truth of God's word and lives in a generous spirit of fellowship, would be rather easy to love.

We must be clear at this point: the upward and inward purposes of the church do not constitute a comprehensive overview of the reason for the church's existence, nor do these purposes fully express the content of the church's mission. In other words, Christ is not building his church solely so that we would worship God and enjoy fellowship with other Christ followers. If that were the case, then Jesus' statement about the gates of hades being powerless against the church[48] would be meaningless. If Acts 2:42 was all that Luke gave to describe the activities of the nascent church, then one could argue for a more isolated posture between the church and culture. But when we read to the end of that paragraph, we see the church "having favor with all the people. And the Lord added to their number day by day those who were being saved."[49] In other words, the *outward* purpose of the

45. Acts 2:42.

46. Acts 4:34–35.

47. Stott, *The Living Church*, 27.

48. Matt 16:18.

49. Acts 2:47.

church was clearly a vital component of the life of the first-century church. Its outward purpose flowed naturally, or perhaps better said, supernaturally, out of the upward and inward purposes. In looking carefully at the early church's ministry in relation to their surrounding culture, we cannot help but notice that the outward purpose that consumed them was *not* primarily to make the world a better place. Its outward purpose was first and foremost to make disciples; it was to do the work of evangelism.[50]

But we must avoid the pendulum swing of imbalance. To use the fulfillment of the great commission as an excuse for a woeful lack of involvement in social and justice issues or acts of relief, mercy, and compassion is to violate Christ's mandate for his church in relation to the world. By the same token, "such ministries of mercy to the world should never become a substitute for genuine evangelism . . ."[51] I will say more on this in the following chapter.

Ray Bowman and Eddy Hall have provided some wisdom and insight that, I am sure, helped create thoughtfully designed and structured church buildings.[52] However, the closing paragraph of their third chapter, "The Myth of Sacred Space," contains vestiges of an egregious misunderstanding for the reason of the church's existence. As it turns out, the authors' whole approach to church building design is based upon a conviction that "the church's mission is to minister to people in Christ's name."[53] Speaking on the role of the built environment, in relation to the mission of the church, they go on to say:

> If our focus is truly on people rather than buildings, that reality will shape the kinds of buildings we design, how we use them, how much we spend on them, and how much time, energy, and money we keep free for the real work of the church: meeting people's needs.[54]

It is their last statement that I find particularly distressing. If we see the function of the church primarily as a repository of ways and means to meet needs, then we will create churches that serve that function. This is a consumeristic paradigm. Our orientation must be more than a missional paradigm that, while not ignoring the inward or upward orientation, is

50. Matt 28:18–20.

51. Grudem, *Systematic Theology*, 868.

52. See Bowman and Hall, *When Not to Build*.

53. Ibid., 44.

54. Ibid.

intentional about an outward focus as well. The apostle Peter provides an excellent, concise purpose statement for us in 1 Peter 2:9: "But you are a chosen race, a royal priesthood, a holy nation, a people for his own possession, that you may proclaim the excellencies of him who called you out of darkness into his marvelous light." This is why God the Father is calling us, why Christ is building us, and why the Spirit is uniting and enabling us: to proclaim the excellencies of God. The ways in which we as the church proclaim God's excellencies will vary from context to context, but the purpose itself must always inform the method, not the other way around.

Christ's Love for the Church

Scripture leaves no doubt regarding the depth of Christ's love for the church. One of the metaphors used throughout Scripture to convey the nature of God's relationship with his people is the marriage between a man and his bride.[55] In the New Testament one need only consider Paul's admonition to husbands in Ephesians 5:25–33. In this passage, Paul uses Christ's love for the church as the standard by which husbands are to measure their love for their own wives. Consider the expressions he uses here: loved her; gave himself up for her; that he might sanctify her; having cleansed her by the washing of water and the word, that he might present the church to himself in splendor, without spot or wrinkle, that she might be holy and without blemish.

The evidence of Christ's love for the church is not limited: "for the joy that was set before he endured the cross, despising the shame and is seated at the right hand of the throne of God."[56] His love for us continues even to this day as, seated at the right hand of God, he "indeed is interceding for us."[57] The nature of that love is such that there is nothing in all of creation that has the capacity to separate us from Christ's love.[58] Our ability to conquer any and all challenges hurled our way is provided through Christ's love for us.[59] Throughout this magnificent anthem of praise,[60] Paul speaks of the objects of Christ's love in the plural; Christ loves *us*, not just *me*!

55. See Hosea 1–3; Ezekiel 6, 23; Isaiah 54; Jer. 2:2–3; Mal. 2:14 and Song of Songs.

56. Heb 12:1–2.

57. Rom 8:34.

58. Rom 8:35–39.

59. Rom 8:37.

60. The entire chapter (Romans 8) is well worth the effort to memorize.

Christ's love for the church can be summed up as an act of commitment and self-giving, as opposed to an emotion. The motivation behind this choice is so that the church, his bride, would be holy and glorious, without blemish. Despite the many wrinkles and blemishes that continue to characterise the church, Christ suffered for us, his bride. I am intrigued and too often given cause for concern at how the church's blemishes are exactly what get the most attention. Many books have been published and countless sermons preached that paint a grotesque, impressionistic portrait of the church. Is it any wonder that we as the church have earned the reputation of being the only army on Earth that shoots its own wounded? Am I suggesting that we ignore the prophetic voices that God has raised up among us or pretend that in our present state we as Christ's bride are flawless or that there are no issues needing to be addressed? Not at all! But I am deeply concerned that we are making what *we* are doing or failing to do the focus of our conversations and thoughts. We must not lose sight of what *Christ* is doing and will continue to do in and through his bride. And above all, we must not lose sight that Christ *loves* his church!

How Are We to Love the Church?

How are we to love the church? What are we are to love? How can we be expected to love the church that historically has suffered the internal distress of self-inflicted wounds, that has been at odds with itself, even to the point of animosity and bloodshed? How do we legitimize loving that which has been criticized for being everything from a quaint community that is soon to run out of shelf life to a recalcitrant, oppressive purveyor of paternalistic, xenophobic intolerance?

Let me begin answering these questions by way of stating my own personal convictions. My love for the church is made manifest in a number of ways that are borne out of a conviction that I need other Christians, and that I need to be with them regularly.[61] In fact, I cannot be the Christian I have become without them. I am okay with that need because I am confident in my identity (who I am) and my purpose (why I am here). If I say I love the church, then I will choose to be with those who are members of the body of Christ. I cannot love the church by proxy or from a distance. Of course, it goes without saying that ultimately it is Christ and the fullness of

61. Heb 10:24–25.

his precious Holy Spirit that I need. God has created me in his own triune image in order that I thrive in community.

First of all, our love for the church must not be based upon what the church does for us. It would appear that many people have cooled in their affection for the church due to unfulfilled promises or unmet expectations. The church has failed to meet our needs. But ours is not to be a responsive love. Rather, our love should be a reflection of Christ's love for the church. Our love is to be a self-giving love of choice, an act of the will as well as the heart. We choose to love the church because Christ loved his church in his life and through his death. Loving the church this way does not imply that we turn a blind eye to wrongs or oppressive actions that may be perpetrated by the church.

Second, we must love the church by refusing to budge from a Christ-like standard of holiness. The apostle Paul loved the church this way. Paul did not "resign" from loving the struggling churches in Galatia, whose feeble efforts to resist religious influences of their day would be enough to discourage any founding pastor. Paul loved them deeply, though he did not withhold necessary reprimands, nor was he averse to investing in them at great personal cost: "my little children, for whom I am again in the anguish of childbirth until Christ is formed in you."[62] Loving the church this way does not allow the society or world we live in to determine what constitutes appropriate conduct. Christ has already demonstrated what appropriate conduct should resemble. Christ chose to love and give himself for the church so that we, as his church, may not only get in to heaven but also experience the holiness of heaven within us. Christ's desire for the church is not primarily that we be relevant or prophetic, or that we be compassionate, do justice, and exhibit loving kindness.[63] His desire, indeed his command, is that we be holy![64]

So how do we love the church when we see a member or a group within the body of Christ failing to live in holiness? Do we castigate this person and then walk away in disgust? Perhaps write a book about them? Here is what Paul suggests: "Brothers, if anyone is caught in any transgression, you who are spiritual should restore him in a spirit of gentleness. Keep watch on yourself, lest you too be tempted. Bear one another's burdens,

62. Gal 4:19.
63. Mic 6:8.
64. 1 Pet 1:15–16.

and so fulfill the law of Christ."[65] The "burdens" to which Paul is referring primarily represent transgressions, sins, failures to live holy lives. We love the church by getting our shoulders under the burden of the one who is struggling.

Without question, our love must have as its object the church universal, the global community of all blood-bought Christ followers. But when Jesus exhorted his disciples to love one another as he had already loved them,[66] he was not envisioning a broad-stroke love that cast a global net of acceptance. He was narrowing this admonition down to a relatively small, clearly identifiable community. We cannot wash the feet of the whole universal church nor can we bear the burdens of the church universal, but we can do this for those people we meet week to week.

My Bible college roommate had a poster over his bed of Charles Schultz's character Lucy from the *Peanuts* comic strip in conversation with Charlie Brown. Lucy said, "I LOVE humanity; it's people I can't stand!" Loving the universal church typically presents little or no challenge for us. It is distant and therefore less demanding. But it is within the context of a local fellowship, with whom you have chosen to identify, that your love for the church is going to be demonstrated most powerfully and authentically. It is in the messy, mundane routines and responsibilities of washing the dirt off one another's lives that the world will take notice. It is through those efforts they will say, "Man, these people really do love each other!"

Loving the church will be most challenging for us during the times when the church does not always operate the way we think it should. How do we love someone or something that doesn't function "normally" or effectively? I can think of no personal story that more powerfully illustrates this love than that of a man whom God used to draw me deeper into Christlikeness. This man was Dr. Robertson McQuilkin. He influenced me almost as much as my own father. Dr. McQuilkin was president of Columbia Bible College and Seminary during my tenure there as an undergrad. His wife, Muriel, was one of the most creative, hospitable, fun-loving women I have ever met. Tragically, the onset of Alzheimer's disease in her mid-fifties brought Muriel's effective public ministry to a premature end. Up until that point, she had been a dynamic presence at conferences, on radio, and on television. Dr. McQuilkin found himself in the unenviable, heart-wrenching tension between two callings, his marriage and his ministry. Against the

65. Gal 6:1–2.
66. John 13:34–35.

well-intentioned counsel of godly, trusted friends, he eventually elected to devote himself to the care of his "bride." This choice drastically reduced his public ministry. In an article published at the request of the editors of *Christianity Today*, Dr. McQuilkin shared with sensitivity and transparency the story of his struggle. One particularly moving statement has riveted itself to my heart and mind. Despite the fact that Muriel no longer functioned or behaved the way she had, he said this:

> She is such a delight to me. I don't *have* to care for her, I *get* to. One blessing is the way she is teaching me so much—about love, for example, God's love.[67]

What an image, not only of the extent of Christ's love for his bride, the church, but the love that should be evident among the members of the body of Christ.

John MacArthur put it this way: "If you love the Lord, you love whom the Lord loves. If you really love the Lord, you love the people the Lord loves. You can't love the Lord and be indifferent to the people He loves." Few if any of us would tolerate anyone bad-mouthing our wife, kids, grandkids, or anyone precious to us. Why should we think Christ would respond otherwise when his bride, the church, is maligned or slandered? It is one thing for people outside the church to do such things. In fact, we should almost expect it. But it is disconcerting when we realize how much injury is caused by friendly fire. And all the while the world watches.

A Necessary Dose of Realism

Eugene Peterson coined a phrase that could be applied to our love for the church: "Ecclesiastical pornography." Pornography presents airbrushed images of unreal, unknowable people that in turn foster unrealistic expectations and dissatisfaction with that which is real.[68] Peterson describes how this is played out in the local church:

> *Parish glamorization is ecclesiastical pornography—taking photographs (skillfully airbrushed) or drawing pictures of congregations*

67. McQuilkin, "Living by Vows," 39.

68. I was reminded of Peterson's expression through an excellent blog entitled "Love the Groom, Hate the Bride" by Chris Price (www.groundedinthegospel.com/blog/love-the-groom-hate-the-bride) hosted by a group called Grounded in the Gospel (www.groundedinthegospel.com/blog).

> *that are without spot or wrinkle, the shapes that a few parishes have*
> *for a few short years. These provocatively posed pictures are devoid*
> *of personal relationships. The pictures excite a lust for domination,*
> *for gratification, for uninvolved and impersonal spirituality.*[69]

Similarly, unrealistic, perhaps even unbiblical, assumptions and expectations regarding the nature and mission of the church can and will hinder a person's ability to enjoy a meaningful relationship with a local congregation. If we are waiting for the church to clean itself up and smooth out the wrinkles, and therefore earn our commitment and love, we should instead remember that in loving the church Christ loves *us*!

Does the Church Have a Future?

Failure to be gripped by the nature and mission of the church, and failure to be convinced of Christ's love for the church, will inevitably lead to a failure to love the church. Such failures cannot help but adversely affect our leadership and ministry within and through the church. To what or to whom was Paul referring when he admonished husbands to love their wives "as Christ loved the *church*, and gave himself for her that he might present her to himself without spot or wrinkle or any such thing"?

It would seem that Paul was referring to us, the members of Christ's church. The challenge for us as Christ followers is to refrain from thinking or speaking of the church in the third person, as though it were something or someone distinct from us and our apparently objective vantage point. If we are Christians, we are the church. When we speak of the church we speak of ourselves in company with other Christians under the headship of Christ. The church is bigger than us, but it includes us.

I need to regularly ask myself questions like, "Is what I am doing and even the way in which I am doing it conveying a profound love for the church that is fostered by a biblical concept on the nature of the church and an understanding of Christ's love for the church, his bride?" As a husband I am clearly called to love my wife the way Christ loved the church. I am also called to love the church the way Christ loves the church. How am I to balance these calls?

As leaders in any ministry role, it is essential that we love the church. Why? Because Christ loved the church, and because the effectiveness of our

---

69. Peterson, *Under the Unpredictable Plant*, 22.

leadership in ministry depends on our love. Love for the church is foundational to any ministry that God in his grace entrusts to our care. By failing to love the church our suitability to lead within the church, or any ministry for that matter, is seriously compromised.

Love for the church inevitably entails getting involved in the mess of life. This work is not always convenient, nor is it without cost. Pastors and elders who see their role primarily as administrative, with little or no call for involvement with those we are privileged to lead, need to be reminded of Paul's admonition to the elders of the Ephesian church: "*Pay careful attention* to yourselves and to all the flock, in which the Holy Spirit has made you overseers, to care for the church of God which he obtained with his own blood."[70]

Those of us who are privileged to lead through a teaching or preaching ministry need to remember, "We do our listeners the greatest favor by gifting them with a place in that community, the dizzying privilege of being part of something bigger than just me or my life, a far better destiny than some mere solo adventure with the Divine."[71]

Our consideration of effectiveness in leadership within a ministry context began by orienting our spiritual compasses to the "true north" of loving God with our whole being—heart, soul, mind, and strength. We have seen how that love is made manifest in a consistently deepening love for the Word of God. In this chapter we have only begun to explore the second essential love, namely love for the church. We would do well to remember that church members are at many different junctions in their journey. Some come with a smile pasted on their face, while inside they are so badly hurting they can barely stand. Some who come have recently discovered Christ and his grace, and are hungry to hear from him. Some who come are going through the motions in an attempt to keep up the proper image. Some come who, despite incredible challenges, exude a delightful and infectious joy. Still others who come find little good and feel it is their God-ordained mandate to notify the pastoral team that the sermon was too long and the music too loud! The church is people who are in process with a God-given purpose. But that imperfect assembly of people in process is still the bride of Christ.

As we grow in our love for the church, our theology of the church (ecclesiology) and the practical outworking of that theology can function

70. Acts 20:28 (emphasis added).
71. Howell, *Beauty of the Word*, 43.

in a mutually beneficial way; and then and only then will our skill sets and gifting be used effectively as we lead. We cannot lead effectively in kingdom work with effect unless we love the Lord with all we are, and we cannot do that and *not* love his church. That is impossible. It is not a concept or a paradigm we are called to love. It is not a tradition or denomination or method. Quite simply, we love the church—one person at a time, one day at a time.

For Group Discussion:

1. Discuss some of the changes in the global church that you have witnessed during the past ten years. Do so both in terms of the benefits and liabilities of these changes. What changes have occurred specifically in your local assembly? Discuss the degree to which these changes reflect the nature of the church as discussed in this chapter.

2. What will the church need to be like in the next ten years? What kind of leadership will be necessary for that kind of church to exist?

For Personal Reflection:

1. How would you presently gauge your own personal love for the church?

2. What aspects of the church you attend keep you coming back?

3. Read Galatians 6:1–5 and prayerfully reflect on how you have received that kind of support ministry. How have you contributed the same into the lives of others?

Prayer: *Lord Jesus I thank you for your promise that you are building your church. What a relief to know that it does not depend on us! I thank you too for your incredible love for us as your bride. Forgive me Lord when I allow the failures of others within the church or my own sense of entitlement to blur my vision of what you are doing in and through your church. In those of us who are in the second half of our journey here, rekindle our love for your church even when it changes its methods as necessary in order to engage its culture redemptively. And raise up new generations of leaders who will not lose sight of where we as the church has been and who will truly love your church and, like you, will be willing to give themselves for it. And may all this be done by your grace and for your glory. Amen.*

FOUR

Love for the Lost, My Neighbor: Evangelism Revisited

I MUST CONFESS TO a significant degree of struggle when settling on the title of this chapter. I was torn between two possibilities: love for "the lost" and love for "my neighbor." I was so torn that I opted for both! Both terms, and the concept behind each, can be found in Scripture, particularly in the parables of Jesus. In Luke 15 we find a series of parables of "lost-ness": lost sheep,[1] a lost coin,[2] and a lost son.[3] Earlier in Luke's gospel we have the record of the exchange between Jesus and a lawyer. The lawyer asked a question with regard to the identity of his neighbor.[4] Lost-ness has a certain stigma that many people in our postmodern, post-Christian era may find offensive. "Neighbor" certainly is a more palatable term, and carries less demeaning connotations.

In the previous chapter we considered our love for the church, that is, our fellow Christ followers. We now change our focus to our love for those outside the Christian faith. I will be using the terms "lost" and "neighbor" interchangeably because both apply, though I realize that the term "lost" comes laden with some unfortunate baggage: With a perceived or real sense of arrogance, we Christians have attached this term to unbelievers. But it is a term we must use because the parables in Scripture, referred to above, speak of people in a "lost" state. In other words, we must never get used to or remain unmoved by the *lostness* of the part of humanity who live outside of a relationship with Jesus Christ. Nor must we, as Christ followers,

1. Luke 15:3–7.
2. Luke 15:8–10.
3. Luke 15:11–31.
4. Luke 10:25–37.

ever lose sight of the fact that we too were once lost, a condition that was remedied solely through God's grace and by his mercy to us in Christ. That knowledge categorically should remove any grounds for entitlement in our own hearts.

For a major portion of my pastoral ministry within the local church, one of the biggest areas of struggle I had resided in the whole area of evangelism, the reaching out to lost people. I did not need convincing that evangelism was an important aspect of my ministry. But evangelism was an aspect of ministry I seldom felt confident or competent in doing. I have to think that my personal angst in this whole area had a history. During my high school years I was a member of our youth group at the church in which my dad served as pastor. I, along with a small handful of keeners (an individual eager to demonstrate knowledge or participate enthusiastically in school or church) in our youth group, engaged in a Sunday afternoon activity that took us out into the streets around our church where we stopped people and did some "cold-canvas" witnessing! I hated it. But I did it for two main reasons: (1) a girl I was dating was a real keener at doing this, and; (2) because my dad was the pastor I had an unshakable sense of obligation. Beyond that, somewhere hidden under the numerous layers of less than stellar motivation, I *did have* a concern for people who did not have a relationship with the living Lord Jesus Christ.

If you had asked me if I loved lost people, I probably would have answered with something like, "Of course I love lost people!" But if I were to respond with ruthless honesty I would have had to confess, when it came right down to it, that no, I did not love lost people—at least not to the degree that I was willing to risk misunderstanding, ridicule, or rejection in an effort to have a conversation about the things that really mattered in life. I just liked being liked too much! In addition, and sadly the main reason, was that I had very few lost friends. Lots of lost acquaintances, but friends? Hey, I didn't have time. And when I became a pastor, feeding and leading a small but growing congregation of Christians consumed the majority of my time and energy!

When I think back on my struggle as a teenager and as a pastor, I see a young man who did want to be effective evangelistically. I see a young man who did want to love lost people. But I also see a young man who should have been more involved but wasn't. So why the struggle? I believe my problem lay in the fact that I had a flawed view of two vital elements of evangelism. What I needed was a clear view of (1) a biblical view of what the gospel really is, and; (2) a biblical view of what evangelism is.

Love for Lost People Must Be Rooted in a Biblical View of the Gospel

What is the essence of the good news, the gospel of Jesus Christ? Unless our fundamental concern is that people come to faith in Christ in order to avoid the horrendous perils of hell (as indescribably terrible as that is—unless, that is, one drifts over to an annihilationist position),[5]) then our concern for these folks is likely to fluctuate like the weather! If, by contrast, salvation is primarily a matter of what Dallas Willard refers to as "a gospel of sin management,"[6] regarding heaven and hell—both are out there somewhere, sometime in the future—we have missed something of profound significance both in terms of understanding and experience.

The good news of the gospel reminds us that we are not waiting for fullness of salvation; we have been promised it now. Furthermore, the gospel or good news message about salvation affects not only the spiritual dimension of a person's life but the whole person, body, soul, and spirit; and encompasses a person's whole life, past, present, and future. My struggle with evangelism was rooted in a truncated view of the gospel, a view that addressed one's *past* sins and failures along with God's remedy for past sins through the death of Christ on the cross; and second, one's *future* destiny, God's promise of eternity with him in heaven. What was missing, both in my own personal convictions and experience as well as my conversations with lost people, was the *present* component of the gospel message. The announcement of good news at the birth of Jesus was not just that he would save his people from their sins, but that his name would also be Immanuel, that is, God is with us—now!

The moment any of us come to the cross, accept the grace of God's gift in and through Christ, we immediately enter the position of fullness of salvation. The apostle Paul put it this way: "For if while we were enemies we were reconciled to God by the death of his Son, much more, now that

5. Basically, the belief that upon death a person ceases to exist. There is no post-mortem consciousness. Some believe this is the end of all humanity; whereas others within the Christian community believe this state of "nonexistence" awaits only those who die rejecting God's gift of salvation through Christ.

6. Willard, *Divine Conspiracy*, 35–59.

we are reconciled, shall we be saved by his life."[7] That phrase "shall be saved by his life" is not written in the future tense, referring to something yet to come. Another way of saying it is "we shall be *being* saved." (on-going-ly). I do wonder sometimes if we have allowed our eschatology to foster a Christian spirituality that is alarmingly reminiscent of Gnostic spirituality. Such an eschatology holds that present reality is but a necessary phrase through which we must pass, anticipating the ultimate emancipation from the fallen state of this body and world in which we live.

As a ministry leader, there is also a subtle danger that comes with becoming so involved with ongoing ministries to Christ followers that we, as leaders, allow our existing ministry to be an excuse for mediocrity when it comes to loving lost people. Mediocrity can take many forms. If you are tired out because of your daily work, then it will be a challenge for you to invite people into a life with Christ. Or if the main or only exciting aspect about your own personal salvation message is that the past is forgiven and the future promises heaven, then you must convince people that they need a remedy for their sin beyond what they can muster through their own sincerity and efforts.

In all honesty, it could be argued that failures in helping people embrace a life with Christ stem from us, leaders in ministry, not living in the exquisite fullness of salvation right now, that is, "Christ in you the hope of glory."[8] But the reality is that our salvation is all encompassing. That is, through Christ's sacrifice God forgives our past, gives hope for the future, and also provides a super abundant life and grace for the present. N. T. Wright puts it so well: "We are saved not as souls, but as wholes."[9] To that I must add what my pastor, Dr. Clyde Glass, says: "You cannot commend what you do not cherish." Before we can witness effectively we have to be convinced that we have a testimony worth sharing. In other words, we must be convinced in our own personal experience that the gospel really is good news.

I think that sometimes we as Christ followers lose sight of, or fail to be gripped by, the fact that we were once lost. This recognition is especially difficult for those of us who were brought up in Christian homes—especially for those of us who have somehow bought into the lie that unless you have survived horrible experiences, and subsequently have been redeemed

7. Rom 5:9–10.

8. Col 1:27.

9. Wright, *Surprised by Hope*, 199.

from the dregs of a debauched life, that you really have nothing that could command the interest of anyone! This flawed way of seeing places *us* at the center of the salvation story, and in so doing detracts from what a testimony really is, and ultimately what the gospel is.

This whole misconception has been exacerbated by the parade of celebrities who the church puts on display. During my college years, I vividly remember sitting next to a former Hell's Angel in one of my classes. His name was Rick, and he sported four tattoos of spiders on his arms. These tattoos were amazing and grotesque, and for me they made concentrating on church history challenging, to say the least! Rick's story truly was amazing: He was miraculously delivered from bondage, making an escape from a community that normally only allowed its members to exit in a body bag. In addition, he survived a four-year addiction to heroine. Rick *really* was *lost* until God rescued him, not only from hell in the future but from a horrific life in the present.

There was a major part of me that was deeply thrilled to know that *my* God was both willing and able to bring about such incredible, powerful change in a person's life. He had obviously done so in Rick's life. God's demonstration of power and love awed me. But there was another part of me that couldn't resist comparing my story with his. As long as I kept myself as the center of my story, and Rick as the center of his, I found nothing but profound discouragement because the comparison was laughable. It is no wonder that the apostle Paul refused to compare himself with other religious people and warned his readers against doing the same: "But when they measure themselves by one another and compare themselves with one another, they are without understanding."[10] Eugene Peterson in *The Message* put it this way: "But in all this comparing and grading and competing, they quite miss the point."[11] Like so many, I had missed the point of a testimony and the role that my testimony played in my witnessing.

So then what is the point? The point is that effective witnessing or personal evangelism is not up to you, and ultimately has nothing to do with the life you lived prior to coming to faith in Christ. It has everything to do with *Christ* and the life he is now living in and through you. In my case, I was and am as needy of Christ's saving life as my former Hell's Angel classmate, Rick! Without belittling or minimizing the miracle of God's grace in the lives of people like Rick, the essence of his salvation story is no greater

10. 2 Cor 10:12.

11. Peterson, *The Message*, 385.

or more spectacular than God's work of grace in my life—a grace that kept me from ever having to be delivered from such a life.

I fear we run the risk of getting used to the gospel and losing the sense of wonder with respect to what the gospel means.[12] When we elect or allow ourselves to become the center of our own salvation story, comparison with others and their journey is virtually inevitable, and the results are far from redemptive. The wonder of salvation has nothing to do with who *we* are or were, or will be. The wonder of our salvation story has everything to do with *Christ*.

The apostle Paul reminded the believers in Rome that "All have sinned and fall short of the glory of God."[13] The word Paul used for *sinned* could be translated as "missed the mark." The image used is that of an archer shooting his arrow at a target and missing. Our tendency is to default into a comparative mode, and then falsely console ourselves with thoughts like, "Well, yes of course I have missed the mark, but he or she has *really* missed the mark!" Whether we miss the mark by an inch or miss by shooting in the exact opposite direction, we miss the target. There are no degrees of missing the mark.

Why is this important in terms of developing our love for our neighbor? This is vital because it keeps our perspective anchored to the reality that there is no one we will ever be privileged to encounter who needs Christ more or less than we, ourselves, do. That I was born to missionary parents and raised in a home dedicated to the service and glory of Christ in no way makes me less needy than my former classmate and Hell's Angel, Rick, for the simple fact that we had both missed the mark—period!

The other side of this wonderful truth is that Rick did not need any more faith than me to receive forgiveness and cleansing. He did not have to get himself to a certain degree of acceptability before the process of regeneration could begin. As ministry leaders, we fail our neighbors and ourselves when we focus on the object of salvation, which is ourselves, more than the author of salvation, which is Christ. Rick and I have equally amazing testimonies of salvation because (I think I have already said this!) the reality is the story of our salvation has nothing to do with us, but everything to do with Christ.

---

12. For an excellent treatment of recapturing the wonder, see Zacharias, *Recapture the Wonder*, (Nashville: Integrity Publishers, 2003).

13. Rom 3:23.

In case I have left the wrong impression, it is important that I make something very clear. I am not for a moment belittling or minimizing the wonder of God's miracle-working grace in the life of someone like Rick. With all my heart I rejoice that the God I worship performs miracles that defy scientific or rationalistic explanation! Rick's deliverance from the life that he once lived and my having been spared ever living such a life are both expressions of the unfathomable grace of God. Our past does not determine or guarantee our present or future. The wonder of the good news, the gospel, is that God's grace is bigger than our past and our future. His grace is also more than sufficient for our present.

Loving my neighbor and in particular my lost neighbor who does not have a relationship with Christ can unnecessarily and effectively be hindered by a perceived gap between us. If we believe that the gospel is anthropocentric, that is, centered on humanity (humanity's sin, humanity's fall, humanity's redemption, and so on), as opposed to believing that the gospel is theocentric that is, centered and founded on the work of God through Christ, more likely than not we will foster a love for our neighbor that is anemic and inconsistent. Setting our sights on the needs of humanity, of how far we have fallen from God's original design, provides us with enough latitude to place our neighbors outside the reaches of God's grace.

A common fallout from adhering to an anthropocentric view of the gospel is an annoying, relentless sense of guilt: we feel that God is always unsatisfied with our performance. Living under the influence of the misguided anthropocentric concept of the gospel leads one to strive to live a holy life, largely on one's own effort, and as a means of avoiding God's wrathful hand of discipline. But the good news of the gospel is that we are able to live holy lives that are pleasing to God. By adhering to a theocratic view of the gospel we can receive his grace and favor simply because he gives them to us. Holy living, or sanctification, then becomes a vehicle of expressing our love for the Lord. Only the gospel can bring freedom from this sort of guilt. No religion can do this.

Effectiveness in loving our neighbor, then, is not enhanced by dwelling on those we are called to love but on the wonder of the gospel itself, the good news of God's unfathomable grace to us in Christ. A second critical area that is essential to the nourishment of an effective love for our neighbor is a biblical understanding of how that message is to be conveyed. In other words, we must have a proper perception of evangelism.

Love for Lost People Must Be Rooted in a Biblical View of Evangelism

I have had the joy of being in ministry long enough to have witnessed some significant shifts in evangelism within the Christian church. During the 1970s, for instance, I received training in two methodologies that, ultimately, the Lord saw fit to bless in wonderful ways over the years. The first is *Evangelism Explosion*. This methodology grew out of the vision of James Kennedy, pastor of Coral Ridge Presbyterian Church in Fort Lauderdale, Florida. The second methodology is a little, yet highly effective, tract known as the *Four Spiritual Laws*. It was designed by Bill Bright, president of Campus Crusade for Christ. Both of these methodologies have provided thousands of Christians with an effective means of sharing their faith and introducing people to the good news of Christ.

During the 1970s, these methodologies and others like them inspired me to understand evangelism as being, primarily, a competition or battle for hell-bound souls. This way of thinking led me to completely lose sight of who the enemy was. I assumed an adversarial posture toward those I was hoping to win. The people to whom I was "witnessing" often represented little more than an argument to be won. Thus, I needed an approach to apologetics that was intent on dismantling false views that opposed my Christian positions. The people I was attempting to "witness" to tragically became a project to be completed, or worse an enemy to be overcome. But the last thing they were in my mind was a friend to be loved. Friendship takes time and can easily get complicated, indeed inconvenient.

Witnessing or Evangelizing: Which Is It?

During the early years of my pastoral ministry I attended a training seminar for pastors. We were asked to write the names of ten unsaved people with whom we were developing friendships that could naturally lead to conversations about the Lord. Out of the sixty or so pastors in attendance, if I recall correctly, none could complete the assignment.

Shortly after that seminar, a book by Joe Aldrich entitled *Lifestyle Evangelism*[14] was published. This title proved to be more controversial than Aldrich had intended. He provided an approach to evangelism that was not truth or argument based. Instead, he provided a highly relational approach

14. Aldrich, *Lifestyle Evangelism*.

that many ministry leaders were not comfortable using. The concept was straightforward: you evangelized, that is proclaimed the good news, not by persuasion or compelling argument, but by the way you lived your life and by learning how to be friends with people. For many ministry leaders it meant liberation from the pressure of having to "close the deal" that we had read into the Evangelism Explosion and Four Spiritual Laws methods. Ministry leaders simply had to be friends with someone. Most ministry leaders, like me, could do that—with Christians. But with a lost person? That was another story!

Aldrich's whole approach received some criticism because it seemed to ask Christians to spend too much time being friends with people, and not enough time telling people about the good news in Christ. This is an interesting criticism. It brings to mind a phrase attributed to St. Francis of Assisi: "Preach the Gospel; use words if necessary." Mark Galli, author of the book, *Francis Assisi and His World*,[15] stated in an article in *Christianity Today* that it is very unlikely Francis ever said such a thing.[16] Moreover, from what we know of his life and ministry he likely would not agree with it! Regardless of who might have said it originally, this statement is problematic because it is very difficult to sustain with Scripture. While we can appreciate the sentiment behind the statement (whoever said it originally!), too many of us as Christ followers unfortunately emphasize *living* the gospel at the expense of *speaking* the gospel. There should be a consistent degree of integrity between our words and actions. Who can argue with that?

Eventually, a lifestyle that emphasizes actions over words bumps up against such passages as Romans 10:9: "because if you confess with your mouth that Jesus is Lord and believe in your heart that God raised him from the dead, you will be saved"; and the words of Jesus himself: "So everyone who acknowledges me before men, I also will acknowledge before my Father who is in heaven, but whoever denies me before men, I also will deny before my Father who is in heaven" (Matt 10:32–33). A Christian who has a passion to see people come into a living, transforming relationship with Christ must use words. "For everyone who calls on the name of the Lord will be saved. How then will they call on him in whom they have not believed? And how are they to believe in him of whom they have not heard? And how are they to hear without someone preaching?"[17]

15. Galli, *Francis of Assisi and His World*.
16. Galli, "*Speak* the Gospel."
17. Rom 19:13–14.

Difficult words, indeed. We may resist them by saying, "evangelism is not my gift; I'm not a one-a-day-Ray!"[18] In all honesty, it used to be easy for me to excuse my lack of evangelistic engagement and effectiveness by reasoning that I was not gifted as an evangelist.[19] But then I came to accept the fact that although evangelism may not be my spiritual motivational gift, it still is and always will be my mandate, my commission and not an option! When we look in Acts 1:8, one of the great commission passages, we must notice what it does *not* say: "But you will receive power when the Holy Spirit has come upon you and you will do evangelism, or you will just hang out with lost people." No, it says "you will *be* my witnesses . . ." Witnessing is a matter of *being*. Witnessing is a way of life that is empowered by the fullness of the Holy Spirit. Put another way, the good news of salvation is concerned with your whole being—body, soul, and spirit.

At the risk of splitting hairs, I contend that witnessing and doing the work of an evangelist (as Paul admonished his young son in the faith, Timothy),[20] are not necessarily the same. They may well be motivated by the same desire to see people experience the good news of God's saving grace in Christ. Witnessing to the work of God's grace in our life can occur to a limited degree through the manner in which we live our lives. But evangelizing, proclaiming the good news of God's saving grace, is explicit and requires the clarity that only *words* can express. Providing health services to the sick, food for hungry people, or relief into needy situations are wonderful and effective means of bearing witness to the love of God. While these services may be the overflow of the transforming power of the gospel in a person's life, such actions are not the gospel. In and of themselves they are inadequate in helping people see that their greater need is the sin that separates them from God, and that the one and only remedy is for them to repent[21] in faith[22] in response to God's own provision in the substitutionary sacrifice of his son, the Lord Jesus Christ. Actions cannot declare that; only words can.

18. This is a moniker given to a dear friend of mine. And this friend, in his gentle, loving, and very consistent way, has lead more people to Christ through one-on-one encounters than anyone else I know.

19. Eph 4:11–12.

20. 2 Tim. 4:5.

21. Acts 3:19–20.

22. Eph 2:8–9.

My son, Tim, gave me the following image that conveys the point I am trying to make. He said, "Imagine if the evening news was presented by a game of charades! It might be funny, but the interpretation could be messy!" The reality is that there are many, many people who demonstrate amazing acts of compassion but who share no sympathies whatsoever with Scripture, or specifically the good news of Christ.

Using words in the process of evangelizing, however, requires that we do much more than learn appropriate and accurate content. We must evangelize with compassion and conviction; we must effectively communicate the good news from the heart. It is not a matter of *information*; it is *transformation*. Solomon reminds us that it is out of the heart that the issues of life come.[23] Words that are going to be effective in evangelism must come from a heart that has been transformed by the gospel being shared.

We are prone to overlook some of the specifics in the Acts 1:8 account of Christ's commission to his disciples. The widening circles (Jerusalem, Judea, Samaria, and the ends of the Earth) remind us that evangelism is to occur in places that are familiar to us. For most of the disciples, this familiar place likely would have been Judea. But evangelism must also be engaged in places that represent opposition and risk. For the disciples such a place was Jerusalem, the location where the whole conspiracy against Jesus originated. For many of us today, evangelism challenges us to live evangelistically among those who are different from us or who represent those who are most difficult to love. These people may even be the most resistant to the gospel message. (For the disciples this would clearly have been among the Samaritans.) But, let us also remember that Jesus tells us to evangelize to "the ends of the Earth." We, like the disciples, are to go to places we have never been and which we likely know little or nothing.

A legitimate question at this point is this: Are the directives Jesus gave his disciples in Acts 1:8 meant to be *prescriptive* of how the universal church is to function across the borders of time and culture, or are they meant to be *descriptive* of what was to be the disciples' experience within the context and timeframe of their lives and ministry? I would argue that there is a prescriptive component to the Great Commission for us, not in the literal sense of starting in the city of Jerusalem and working out through the regions of Judea and Samaria (such territorial borders have morphed over the centuries). Rather, I see this as prescriptive in the sense that like those first disciples we as the church have been given the mandate of being

23. Prov 4:23.

witnesses to the good news of Christ in contexts with which we are familiar as well as those that may represent risk, resistance, and even the unknown. Millard Erickson is strongly convinced that the church needs to be working in all of these areas. "If it does not, it will become spiritually ill, for it will be attempting to function in a way its Lord never intended."[24]

In 1938 when my parents left the comforts of home in Toronto to live among the Ngumbai people in French Equatorial Africa (today known as Chad), the term "mission field" was used in the limited sense to refer to countries beyond the shores of North America. Over time the scope of this term changed. For example, in one church where I was privileged to preach, there is a banner across the door as you exit the sanctuary that reads, "You are now entering the mission field." The missionary frontier is now local, within meters of the North American church's front door. The "ends of the Earth" have come to us. Maybe what that means in terms of witnessing and evangelizing is that some of us need to seize the day of opportunity and learn Spanish or Mandarin or Arabic or one of several other languages that are used cross-culturally within our own borders!

The Lost Art of Listening

The thought of venturing with the gospel into areas with which we are unfamiliar or would prefer to avoid has caused some of us to scramble for new methodologies. We invent methods to reach Gen Xers or Gen Y people (or Millennials) or whatever the group *à jour* might be! I would suggest that a lot of us don't need another method or argument or means of *telling* people about the good news of the gospel. In order to become effective in reaching groups unfamiliar to us, we need to resurrect one of the most underused components of the whole evangelistic endeavor. I am talking about two external organs that hang on either side of our head—our ears. Most of the training I received in evangelism was designed to help me know what to *say*. What I have had to learn the hard way, often taking stumbling small steps, is how to say nothing and *listen*! There was good reason why James admonished his readers to be "quick to hear, slow to speak, slow to anger."[25] Listening is an absolutely necessary complement to our words and lifestyle. Why should people listen to me if I give the impression that I have little or no interest in listening to them? The gospel is always right,

24. Erickson, *Christian Theology*, 1054.

25. Jas 1:19.

always relevant. Unfortunately, the timing and the manner in which we speak it is not.

Effectively listening to another person, however, takes time. It can be frustrating. One of the greatest challenges for many of us is having the willingness and ability to listen to another person in order to *understand* the person speaking. If, while listening, we are mentally loading our guns, as it were, for our next barrage of argumentation, the possibility of understanding the other person, and therefore being able to communicate effectively, is greatly reduced. A willingness to listen in itself can convey respect for another person. Among other things it demonstrates a willingness to concede that this other person just might have something of equal value to contribute, something from which we might even benefit.

Reflecting on my own journey as a leader in ministry, I would have to say that one of the main reasons I failed in this respect was due to fear; fear that, given enough time, the person I was "witnessing" to might present an argument or raise a question for which I had no adequate response. As I have come to learn, when that situation occurs we may find ourselves on the defensive, a position in which we no longer have control over setting the direction of the conversation. What I discovered, through willingly taking the risk to listen, was that not all people who were within the circle of my lost acquaintances were adamantly antagonistic toward the Christian faith or Scripture. But they did have honest, searching questions and objections that deserved a hearing and a response.

At this point, I need to clarify what I am *not* saying. I am not saying that our willingness to listen should invest secular culture with the same authority as Scripture. Final authority of Scripture must be guarded. Rather, we must listen to culture so we can understand culture, and thus have a better concept of how the truth of Scripture can be communicated effectively within that culture. Equally important is that listening carefully, and with the Spirit's discernment, also makes room for us to catch a glimpse of what God might already be doing in a given person's world. I have come to believe *God is never doing nothing; he is always doing something.*

There is another fear as well, a concern that our willingness to listen to the culture or to an individual will unnecessarily cause us to risk compromising the authority and integrity of the gospel. Depending on the strength and depth of your own grasp of the gospel, coupled with the intensity of your conversation partner's objections or arguments, compromise is always possible. But it need not be assumed as inevitable. In my own experiences, there have been occasions when a conversation with a person outside the Christian faith has forced me to revisit some of my long held convictions, only to have those beliefs strengthened. But God has also graciously used conversations and insights from some of my unsaved friends to correct some of my blind spots in the cultures that surround me, and even correct my own theology. Simply, these conversations took me out of the cultural context to which I had grown accustomed. Scary? Yes, of course. But such experiences are sometimes absolutely essential if we are to effectively demonstrate our love for our neighbor. Tim Keller puts it so well:

> When we interact with people from other cultures and social settings, we find our particular distortions being challenged. So while gospel communicators should seek to correct their *hearers'* cultural beliefs with the gospel, it is inevitable that contact with a new culture will also end up correcting the *communicators'* understanding of the gospel."[26]

While I was a student at Capernwray Bible School in England, I was given the opportunity to "give my testimony" in a coffee house. This, I did; and later that evening while I was hanging out and having coffee with the young people in attendance, a young guy asked me if we could chat. He had a question about something I had said during my talk: I had referred to a very significant occasion when God "really spoke to me," a phrase I had used on numerous occasions within a Christian context. Without being antagonistic or facetious, he wanted to know what God's voice sounded like! After all, I had insinuated that I had heard it! Most of my Christian friends would have understood what I had meant by that particular phrase, but this young man didn't. I found that I did not have the sufficient vernacular apparatus to convey to him what that meant. What that conversation helped me to understand, as never before, was that my concept of how God sometimes communicates to us today was so radically foreign to the mind and experience of my conversation partner that, even though we shared the same mother tongue, I couldn't communicate clearly to him the truth of God's work in my life.

There is one and only one gospel. But there is not a one-size-fits-all method or paradigm for presenting that good news. By stating that the Bible has no expressions of the gospel that are entirely culture free, one is not required to relinquish a commitment to absolute truths within Scripture.[27] If

26. Keller, *Center Church*, 103.

27. See Timothy Keller's excellent input on the matter of contextualization in chapter

you develop a good listening ear as part of your evangelistic efforts, you will simply increase the likelihood that the method you do use will be effective. However, if in your listening all you basically do is look for a breakdown in the other person's defense, so that you can launch your prepackaged assault, the conversation will very quickly take on the competitive flavor of a joust in which each of you tries to knock the other off your intellectual horse. Occasionally, arguments may be won this way, but people seldom, if ever, will be.

One of my seminary professors, Martin Sanders, developed the habit of frequently going to happy hour at a bar called the Jolly Roger. This bar was within walking distance from our campus. He would order his soft drink and simply join in the conversations that would ensue. His plan was not to witness, as I had been taught. Instead, his intent was to make sure he did not leave that place without presenting the gospel, or what we called "the plan of salvation," to at least one person. His main concern was not to manipulate the conversation toward "spiritual things." Rather, he wanted to listen prayerfully and with discernment in order to understand the hearts and mindsets of the Jolly Roger patrons, none of whom would likely darken the door of any church, much less attend one of his seminary classes!

It took a lot of time and several visits to the Jolly Roger before one of the regulars took the initiative to broach the topic of God. It took time for them to be convinced that Martin was concerned about them as people, not as projects. Martin made the effort to listen, and he made the time to listen.

By contrast, we ministry leaders often transform such conversations into a divine appointment. That is, we believe that our witness could be the only one that another person will ever have before going into a Christless eternity. I have known the weight of self-inflicted eschatological pressure: Jesus could come at any moment, and if I don't share Christ with them, at this time, I could be responsible for their damnation. As I mentioned at the outset of this chapter, I never want to take the lostness of humanity lightly. But a mindset that crosses over from divine urgency to human panic suggests that evangelism is entirely up to us, and thus fails to reflect the fact that the Lord Jesus loves whoever we are talking to more than we ever could. By willingly taking humanity's place on the cross, Jesus already has moved heaven and earth to demonstrate the depth and breadth of his love and grace. He is not wringing his hands, waiting anxiously for us to

---

8, "Balanced Contextualization," in his book *Center Church*.

get out there and reach lost people! But he is graciously extending to us the invitation to be a part of what he is doing.

One of the most effective ways we can demonstrate our love for lost people, then, is to expose them to the truth of God's amazing, saving grace in the finished work of Christ. Inherent in that whole process there must be a willingness to listen to unsaved people, for the purpose of understanding who they are. We may be soundly convinced of their need—they are sinners who are lost and therefore need God's gracious work of redemption in their lives—but be woefully oblivious to where they are emotionally, intellectually, financially, or physically. Jesus was concerned about people holistically, not just their souls, and so should we. Only in this way will we be in the position to allow the Holy Spirit to guide us in a clear and compelling presentation of the gospel that will be strategically effective in any particular context.

Our love for lost people has to be rooted in a biblical understanding of the gospel. For some of us that may mean unlearning some concepts that are informed more by humanistic reasoning than biblical truth. Our love for lost people also has to be rooted in a biblical understanding of what evangelism really is.

Jesus and the Lost Neighbor

Jesus describes the workings of everyday evangelism through his well-known parable of the Good Samaritan.[28] This was a story Jesus told in answer to the question, "Who is my neighbor?"[29] Note that the notion of loving our neighbor as ourselves is cited directly or alluded to no less than six times in the New Testament.[30] In Jesus' parable it is a Samaritan, a man from a group of people despised by the average Jewish person, who refused to be restrained by the existing racial, intellectual, and spiritual borders of his day and penetrated a world of steep prejudice in order to engage in concrete acts of costly love.[31] In telling this story, Jesus demonstrates that

28. Luke 10:30–37.

29. Luke 10:29.

30. See, for example, Matt 5:43–44; Rom 12:14–21; Jas 2:8–14; 1 John 3:17–18.

31. It is difficult for those of us who live in cultures where oppressive prejudices are reasonably contained, or at least politically managed temporarily, to enter into the pathos of what was being conveyed here.

authentic neighbor love knows no borders. It demands we love our neighbor with our heart, soul, mind, and strength.

Love for lost people, as demonstrated through the life of the Samaritan in Jesus' parable, does not generate a new set of rules to be obeyed. Rather it extends an invitation to us to participate in what God has already done and continues to do—love the unlovely, the unworthy, the oppressed and abused. There is no ambiguity with respect to what neighbor love is to look like or include: forgiveness, kindness, providing food and shelter, forbearance, generosity, and more. God has extended every one of these loves, without exception, to us as humans. This kind of love is not earned. God loved us while we were yet enemies.[32] What enemy has ever *earned* love? Earlier, in Luke 6:32, 35, Jesus reminded his listeners in no uncertain terms that loving those who already love us or doing good to those who do good to us is shallow and merits no credit whatsoever. Our love for our neighbor has one and only one standard by which it must be gauged, and that is the love of God for us. Loving lost people, therefore, is going to be costly, and can often prove to be messy. It might even cost us our life. Are you up for that?

Twice in my life I have been impacted by examples of people who paid the ultimate price of loving the lost. I was only six years old at the time, but I can still recall the Sunday evening service at Oakwood Baptist Church in Toronto when we were informed of the martyrdom of five missionaries at the hands of Waodani warriors in the jungles of Ecuador. This tribe had been nicknamed "Aucas," meaning naked savages, because of the unparalleled violence with which they treated any and all intruders.[33] Even at a very young and tender age, my life was profoundly impacted by the willingness of some to love the lost, even to the point of death.

Many years later in January 1981, an example of this love was brought even closer home when a good friend and classmate of mine, Chet Bitterman, was kidnapped in the city of Bogota, Colombia, by a terrorist group.[34] Chet and his wife, Brenda, along with their two daughters, Anna and Esther, were linguists working in Colombia in an effort to get Scripture into the language of people who needed to know the gospel. After several

32. Rom 5:10.

33. Steve Saint, son of Nate Saint who was one of the five murdered missionaries in 1956, has written a gripping account of his return to the people who took his father's life. See Steve Saint, *End of the Spear*, Carol Stream, IL: Salt River, 2005.

34. A fellow classmate of ours, Steve Estes, has written a stirring account of Chet's story in the book, *Called to Die*, Grand Rapids, MI: Zondervan, 1986.

tortuous days of convoluted negotiations, Chet was executed with a single bullet to the chest. He loved the Colombian people, including his terrorist captors, even through the final moments of his life. To this day I am still deeply moved by Chet's love for lost people and ask myself what has my love for lost people cost me—seriously?

Loving our neighbor as ourselves is challenging enough as it is. But we have to notice that in his teaching Jesus took it yet a step further. In the upper room,[35] after demonstrating the extent to which he was willing to go in loving his disciples, Jesus says this: "A new command I give you; Love one another. As I have loved you, so you must love one another. By this all men will know that you are my disciples if you love one another."[36] Although this incident took place in the context of the Passover meal celebrated by Jesus and his disciples and did not include others beyond this tight circle, the underlying love principle demonstrated and taught by Jesus here has profound implication for the way in which we extend our love to the lost.

The weight of what Jesus was doing and his subsequent teaching only becomes clear as we understand the significance of Jesus' actions immediately prior. The meaning and power of Jesus choosing to get up, partially disrobe, and wash his disciples' feet is lost on most of us brought up in a Western culture in which foot washing is seldom, if ever engaged. There were very few persons on the social ladder of Jesus' day lower than the one assigned with the responsibility of washing people's feet. The disciples of Jesus knew this, and it was for this reason that none of them took the initiative to lower themselves to such a degree. It was also very likely the reason that Peter recoiled in shock and refused to allow Jesus to wash his feet. His theology of what the Messiah should be like certainly did not include assuming such a humble posture.

Yet Jesus did so without hesitation, and he used this action to illustrate two things. First, he communicated the fact that there was nothing that the culture of their day considered too low or demeaning that he would not do on their behalf; that is, how much he loved them—and is likely what the apostle John had in mind when he introduced this whole scenario with "when Jesus knew that his hour had come to depart out of this world to the Father, *having loved his own who were in the world, he loved them to the end*."[37] Second, Jesus made it very clear that this was the degree to which

35. John 13–17.
36. John 13:34–35.
37. John 13:1 (emphasis added).

his disciples were to love each other. There is no glamour in this love, nor is there guaranteed benefit in return. This love is not a give and take or a 50/50 arrangement. Entitlement has nothing to do whatsoever with this kind of love.

Self-love, as we will see in the next chapter, seems to come quite naturally for the vast majority of us. But the way Jesus loved his disciples did not come naturally or easily. It was a choice that potentially went against everything that did come naturally. No human has the capacity to love that way, that consistently.

Love for our neighbor, according to Sondra Wheeler, "is the form of human love that most directly and fully imitates the love of God."[38] Jesus' response to the query of what constituted the greatest commandment vividly underscores this. The poignant phrase, "as yourself," a passage found in Leviticus 19:18 that Jesus included as the second greatest commandment, does not represent a command to love oneself. Rather, it is an assumption that such love exists. Jesus' point was that our love for our neighbor should be the same as our love for ourselves. It needs no urging but rather comes as an automatic, self-preserving response. The problem is that as a result of the fall we are no longer wired that way. The natural inclination of self-love that preserves us, as individuals, has remained. The same cannot be said of our love for our neighbor.

Many commentaries have been written on humanity's capacity and willingness to temporarily bracket personal agendas and expend time, energy, and money in an effort to come to the aid of people they have never met. The horrific aftermath of devastation following the 2004 Southeast Asian tsunami and 2005 Hurricane Katrina along the U.S. Gulf Coast are but two salient examples. As wonderful as these unsolicited outpourings of love and concern are, the neighbor love that Jesus was referring to, I would argue, seems to be the more ordinary, mundane love that involves people with whom we rub shoulders on a regular basis. That is, our next-door neighbors. Jesus did not expect us to love our neighbors solely when and because they have need. He expected us to love them for the simple reason that they exist and are somehow a part of our lives.

It is for that reason that I believe the need does not constitute the call; *obedience* constitutes the call. Without question it is often far easier to love neighbors we seldom meet, if ever, than those we cross paths with on a regular basis. The parable of the Good Samaritan demonstrates how

38. Wheeler, *What We Were Made For*, 83.

Jesus leaves no room for ambiguity or wondering with respect to who our neighbor is. Notice he did not tell the story of the good member of the tribe of Benjamin or Judah who loved the wounded pagan Samaritan, the *goyim*!

Neighbor love is distinct from other forms of love such as romantic love, familial affection, or friendship in that there is no reasonable undergirding or foundation; there may be nothing intrinsic to my neighbor's character or situation that attracts me or solicits a response; she may have done nothing to meet any personal need. She just is, and she is my neighbor. Love for my neighbor is not a sprint that lasts for a relatively short season. It is a marathon that takes time and often requires great cost.

We must never lose sight that this is a love that fallen humanity is completely incapable of manufacturing or maintaining over the long haul, that is, as a lifestyle. Holiness or sanctification then is removed from the realm of religious obligation to the much higher supernatural plane of love. It is for this reason that Thomas Aquinas referred to his kind of love as a supernatural virtue.

We love the Lord because he has first loved us.[39] We are to love our neighbor because he exists, which is exactly how the Lord has loved us. No merit, no intrinsic attraction exists on our part. Only we were not even his neighbors; we were his enemies when Christ died for us.[40] This love is one of the main reasons why regular participation in the Eucharist or the Lord's Supper is so essential. The receiving of the elements reminds us how much we have and continue to receive from a loving God that we really don't deserve nor ever could earn.

So How Does This Happen?

God's people have always been aliens and sojourners. Abraham was called by God to leave his homeland and sojourn to a faraway land. Centuries later his descendants were aliens and slaves in the land of Egypt. When Jesus commissioned his disciples, he sent them out *not* to blend into the scenery, but to go as lambs among wolves.[41] Jesus himself knew what it meant to live like an alien even among his own people.[42] So as aliens and sojourners in a culture that is seldom open to the claims of Christ, how do

39. 1 John 4.

40. Rom 5:10.

41. Luke 10:3.

42. Mark 6:4.

we bring the good news of the gospel to bear on the lives of our neighbors in an accessible way?

During the last four decades, in North America particularly, a phenomenon known as the "seeker sensitive" approach has proven very effective in numerous contexts for bringing the unchurched into hearing range with the gospel. Willow Creek Church, under the leadership of lead pastor, Bill Hybels, located in the Chicago suburb of West Barrington, Illinois, is considered by most to be the birthplace of contemporary expressions of seeker sensitive ministries.[43] It is what has been described as an attractional model in that church attenders are encouraged and enabled to invite their "lost" friends to a service that has been designed with the unchurched person in mind. Music during these services is intentionally germane to the tastes of the target audience, and the sermon is crafted in the language of the visitor but is unapologetically clear on a gospel presentation. Whether or not one likes or agrees with the attractional, seeker sensitive model of a ministry like that of Willow Creek Church, one cannot deny the fact that these efforts are borne out of a passionate conviction that lost people matter to God and so should matter to us as the church.

Application at the Local Level

When talking about authentic love for our neighbor, we must bring it down out of the general, ethereal love for a faceless mass of people known as humanity. In other words, we cannot allow our love for the lost to hang in the realm of the ethereal, like Lucy's love for humanity (in the *Peanuts* comic) referred to in the previous chapter. Such a sentiment is much closer to the painful truth than many of us are willing to admit. But loving the lost or loving my neighbor in this way makes huge assumptions: It assumes that we actually know some lost people; that we are developing the kind of relationship with people who need the good news of God's grace; that we strike up conversations as friends; that we do not treat the unsaved as projects. It also assumes that we are making every effort to understand our neighbor as much as we possibly can.

---

43. It needs to be pointed out, however, that seeker sensitive methodologies are not really a twentieth-century phenomenon. Jonathan Edwards was known to use unorthodox methods in an effort to bring people under the influence of the gospel during the Great Awakening.

Let's bring this love down to a more specific, practical, and tangible application within the leadership of the local church. According to the apostle Paul, elders or overseers[44] are to be *hospitable* people,[45] a word that could be translated as "lovers of strangers." Unfortunately, we have tended to limit this hospitality to a truncated concept of opening up one's home for fellowship with the saints. But the kind of hospitality Paul cites as prerequisite to elder leadership assumes a context involving those outside the circle of Christian friends and acquaintances. If we take Scripture seriously and believe it has relevant application to our congregations today, but we are not given to hospitality (that is, we somehow are not involved in the lives of those who need to hear the good news), then we should not be serving as elders leading and caring for the bride of Christ.

I am intrigued how often we have entangled ourselves in discussions over the qualifications of elders such as Paul's insistence that an elder be "the husband of one wife,"[46] or "managing his own household well,"[47] while paying relatively little attention to the other inclusions in Paul's list, such as those that relate to this issue of loving our neighbor. Note that business acumen and the ability to crunch numbers effectively are conspicuously absent from Paul's list. Does this mean that, for instance, those with good business or administrative skill sets and those who are gifted as financial management should not be considered as an elder? By no means, as long as the qualifications that Scripture *does* clearly present as mandatory are evident in a person's life.

Genuine love for lost people is not something we froth up like a good latte. This type of love is something that only Christ himself can do in and for us by the Holy Spirit This kind of love for lost people, a love that requires the enabling fullness of the Holy Spirit, was driven deeply into my heart by the early writings of Dr. Francis Schaeffer, particularly his book *The Church at the End of the 20th Century*.[48] The challenge he gave in the following section is not for the faint of heart:

> In about the first three years of L'Abri all our wedding presents were wiped out. Our sheets were torn. Holes were burned in our rugs . . . It couldn't happen any other way. Drugs came to our place.

44. 1 Tim 3:1 (ESV).

45. 1 Tim 3:2.

46. Ibid.

47. 1 Tim 3:4.

48. Schaeffer, *Church at the End of the 20th Century*.

> People vomited in our rooms . . . How many times have you risked
> an unantiseptic situation by having a girl who might easily have
> a sexual disease sleep between your sheets? We have girls come
> to our homes who have three or four abortions by the time they
> are 17. Is it possible they have venereal disease? Of course. But
> they sleep between our sheets. How many times have you let this
> happen in your home? Don't you see this is where we must begin?
> This is what the love of God means. This is the admonition to the
> elder—that he must be given to hospitality. Are you an elder: Are
> you given to hospitality? If not, keep quiet. There is no use talking.
> But you can begin.[49]

A bit extreme? Does this mean we should all be going out on the
streets and yanking a few homeless people into our homes so they can soil
our sheets and vomit on our carpets? Not necessarily. But what if one of
our children had a struggling friend? Would we have room for them in
our homes as well as our hearts? Now let me say this—exposing any young
children we might have in our homes needs to be weighed carefully and
prayerfully. To do so simply because the need is there may in fact be an act
of presumption or worse, disobedience.

Jesus made it very clear that loving God with our whole person is not
made manifest most effectively in the lifestyle of a hermit. A God-oriented
life does not foster isolation from others. In fact, Jesus stated in no uncertain
terms that the opposite is true by weaving a seamless link between Leviticus
19:18 and Deuteronomy 6. Love for God in and of itself, according to Jesus'
teaching, does not fulfill all the law and prophets. It is love for God and love
for one's neighbor that accomplishes this. "On these two commandments
depend all the Law and the Prophets."[50]

The Greek word that is translated by our English word love here is
agape. This term describes an aggressive, boundless extension of goodwill
to those who have neither earned such love nor have the capacity or perhaps even the willingness to repay. Yet as we love and serve our neighbor
to this degree, we love God. As John Wesley put it, "We are to serve him
(God) in our neighbor; which he receives as if done to himself in person,
standing visible before us."[51] Was not this what Jesus meant when he said,
"Truly I say to you, as you did it to one of the least of these my brothers, you

49. Ibid., 108.

50. Matt 22:40.

51. Wesley, *Works*, 11, 440.

did it to me."[52] However, when we allow that love for our neighbor alone to be the foundation of our ethics or religious activities, we have succumbed to a humanistic paradigm that will inevitably run aground. Love for our neighbor, as I have pointed out earlier, must be organically linked to our wholehearted love for the Lord himself.

I believe the reason for this, in part, is because loving our neighbor as commanded in Leviticus 19:18, and as taught and exemplified through the life and teaching of Christ himself, resides beyond the realm of human capability. Loving our neighbor is complex; it is morally, intellectually, and spiritually challenging. We have a tendency to oversimplify the enormity of this love and too often, like a river wending its way to the ocean, take the course of least resistance. Yet the embodiment of our love for the Lord will be seen no clearer than in our love for our neighbor.

When we consider the example of Jesus in washing his disciples' feet and the radical, aggressive love of the Samaritan in Jesus' parable, we can only conclude that such love is supremely supernatural. But some may wonder what we do with Paul's statement in Galatians 5:14. "For the whole law is fulfilled in one word: 'You shall love your neighbor as yourself.'" Or what about James's statement (2:8)? "If you really fulfill the royal law according to the Scripture, 'You shall love your neighbor as yourself,' you are doing well." Does it not seem that both Paul and James have omitted a significant part of Jesus' response to the religious leaders of his day, namely loving God with our whole being? I would suggest that both of these writers were so well versed in the organic link between our wholehearted love for God and our neighborlove that they knew that the concrete, existential demonstration of our love for God would be clearly manifest in our love for our neighbor.

"Christ does not speak about knowing the neighbor but about becoming a neighbor oneself, about showing oneself to be a neighbor just as the Samaritan showed it by his mercy."[53] Kierkegaard believes that everyone is our neighbor. "To love yourself in the right way and to love the neighbor correspond perfectly to one another; fundamentally they are one and the same thing."[54] In his excellent book, *The Jesus Creed*, Scot McKnight reminds us that "Love, a term almost indefinable, is unconditional regard for a person that prompts and shapes behaviors in order to help that person to

---

52. Matt 25:40.

53. Kierkegaard cited in Jeanrond, *Theology of Love*, 110.

54. Kierkegaard, *Works of Love*, 22.

become what God desires."[55] I have come to believe that people are willing to forgive their leaders a multitude of sins if they are convinced that their leaders love them.

We show ourselves to be true children of God, and therefore demonstrate our wholehearted love for him, in the way we love the lost. We must love them as God has loved us in Christ. Love for our neighbor cannot be separated from our love for God. Jesus made that very clear in his greatest commandment. Because we must love God with all we are, all attempts to love our neighbor that are divorced from a deeply rooted love for God with our whole being are doomed to frustrating, short-lived failure. By the same token, a claim to love God with our whole being that does not flow into a genuine love for our neighbor must be considered suspect at best. Though this kind of love may eventually include an emotional dimension, it certainly does not begin there. This is one kind of love in which rather than feeling our way into new actions, we must act our way into new depths of feeling. We love our neighbor and in particular, lost people, in the very same way God loves us—we *choose* to love them. Love for our neighbor that is divorced from our love for God is nothing more than noble humanistic effort; and love for God divorced from neighbor love is empty, self-centered religion.

Love for lost people that does not address issues of justice and social concern is to present a partial gospel that fails to reflect accurately the message and ministry of Jesus. But by the same token, love for lost people that concentrates solely on social issues to the neglect of a clear presentation of the cross-resurrection elements of the gospel and our inability to remedy the human condition and separation from God, represents an equally truncated gospel. We must be prepared for the fact that a perceived lack of concern for social and justice issues on our part will provide adequate reason for many to disregard us and our gospel.

Love for the Lost—a Corporate Affair

Before I draw this consideration of love for our lost neighbor to a close, I need to emphasize that there is a seamless link between this love and our love for the church. Because salvation is not presented in Scripture as an individual existence but as a new way of living within a new community, it makes sense that we must consider our love for the church prior to

55. McKnight, *Jesus Creed*, 8–9.

considering our love for the lost. A disregard or personal distancing from the church belies not only a flawed ecclesiology[56] but, even more distressingly, a misunderstanding of the gospel itself. Such a gap cannot help but have a direct impact on the effect we can have in the lives of lost people.

The experience of the gospel in any person's life is not limited to the individual plane, but also includes incorporation into the body of Christ, or what Volf calls "a translation of a person into the house of God (*oikos tou theou*) erected in the midst of the world."[57] The apostle Peter emphasizes this incorporation through his use of a series of collective descriptions of who we are as Christians. "But you are a chosen race, a royal priesthood, a holy nation, a people for his own possession . . ."[58] All of these images convey corporate realities as opposed to individual identities. Even the sacraments we observe and cherish, particularly the Lord's Supper and baptism, were not intended to be exercised in solitude. I would argue that, in the same way, loving lost people through any evangelistic effort is not solely an individually based endeavor, but a corporate affair. Without question, the majority of conversations that impact people with the good news will transpire between two individuals, but even those events must envision the incorporation of the individual into a community of like-minded Christ followers.

As people who are created in the image of a triune God—three persons in one essence—it makes sense entirely that our identity and our mission are fundamentally corporate in nature. But it is important to be mindful, as Volf reminds us, that the New Testament Church "was to live an alternative way of life in the present social setting, transforming it, as it could, from within. In any case, the community did not seek to exert social or political pressure, but to give public witness to a new way of life."[59] That alternative way of life Volf refers to is at the core of Jesus' admonition to his disciples; that is, to love one another as he had loved them. People know that they are disciples of Jesus not primarily through their preaching or healing ministries but through the way they relate to other Christ followers, through the way they love each other.[60] Jesus even went further in his high priestly prayer. As described in John 17, he prayed that through unity among Christ

---

56. Ecclesiology is the study or doctrine of the church.

57. Volf, *Captive*, 73.

58. 1 Pet 2:9.

59. Volf, *Captive*, 74.

60. John 13:34–35.

followers the world would come to understand the good news that God the Father loved the world in sending his son, the Lord Jesus.[61]

Our love for our lost neighbor cannot be separate or distinct from our love for our brothers and sisters in Christ, that is, the church. Loving our neighbor, then, is not to be lived out solely on the individual level but on the corporate level as well. For whatever reason, should you chose to distance yourself from fellowship and worshipping with other Christ followers, you have effectively curtailed one of the most significant means of conveying love to your lost neighbor. As leaders in ministry, we need other Christians to be the Christian we have become; likewise, we cannot be as effective in loving our lost neighbour if we are on our own, isolated from fellow believers.

A Matter of Precedence

A final question at this point is this: Should one of these loves—love for our lost neighbor or love for the church—be greater or take precedence over the other? The short answer is, of course, no! One would be very hard pressed to find any Scripture that would provide substantial evidence or support for posturing love for the church over love for the lost, or vice versa. Unfortunately, there is a tendency sometimes to allow concentration on one of these loves to provide excuse for not engaging the other. As leaders in ministry it could be very easy us to become so consumed with attending to the needs and wants of the local saints that our love for our lost neighbors is there in theory, but hardly in praxis.

Effectiveness in the evangelistic endeavor is initially contingent upon a biblical understanding of what the gospel really is, and secondly what evangelism in reality entails. If this is not a settled issue in the hearts and minds of those in leadership positions, then we must not be surprised with anemic demonstrations of love for lost people from our churches. I recognize there are contexts in which ministries are called to face inordinate resistance or outright opposition, resulting in what could be perceived as less than impressive numbers. But, please know my heart in this: churches that have seen the number of conversions and baptisms hover in the few to none range must be willing at least to ask why this might be, and do so by engaging in some self-examination without becoming overly introspective. There may indeed be the realities of spiritual warfare in these churches that

61. John 17:23.

are waging serious interference. If so, these leaders must pray accordingly. But it could also be that leaders of such churches have failed or refused to "get it" as far as what the gospel is essentially and what evangelizing entails.

Just like an airplane needs two wings to fly,[62] our love for our lost neighbors will only be affective when we express that love through the consistent combination of witnessing and evangelizing; that is, living lives that demonstrate the love of God even if that means being sacrificially involved in meeting people's needs and witnessing an unapologetic, grace-filled presentation of truth of the good news. I am left with the impression that, at times, we have created a dichotomy in which loving lost people and telling them about the gospel are polarized as though they were antithetical. Our concern over the offensive nature of topics such as sin, repentance, and exclusive requirement of faith in God's one and only provision for humanity's dilemma has caused us to keep our mouths shut. This is unfortunate. Yet I believe one of the most unloving gestures we can inflict on any lost people is (after loving them with acts of kindness and compassion) we refuse to *tell* them the essence of what makes the gospel good news. The power and wonder of God's love loses significant impact in the absence or avoidance of God's righteous judgment. Leaders, this begins with us! When it comes to loving the lost, loving our neighbors, how is your heart?

For Group Discussion:

1. What kinds of endeavors, though legitimate in themselves, might potentially crowd out or eclipse a clear and consistent presentation of the gospel within Evangelical churches today? What do you think needs to occur in order to avoid that taking place?

2. I distinguish in this chapter between *witnessing* and *evangelizing*. Discuss whether or not you agree with me and why or why not?

For Personal Reflection:

1. What would you say has been your greatest fear or hindrance in loving lost people enough to witness or evangelize, or both?

2. What do think would help you move toward overcoming that fear?

62. Thanks to my long-time friend and colleague Dr. Tim Moore for this analogy.

Prayer: *Gracious, loving Father, forgive me for getting so used to and being so unmoved by the fact that you loved the world, including me, so deeply that you willingly chose the unimaginable—to allow your Son, Jesus, who knew no sin, not only to bear our sin but to be made sin, so that we might be made righteous in him. I confess my inability to conjure up a consistent love for my lost friends and acquaintances. I don't need another method of witnessing or evangelism; I need a renewed heart. I ask you, in Jesus' name, to do that for me—right now. And I ask this by your grace and for your glory. Amen.*

FIVE

Love for One's Self: Narcissism or Necessity?

JOHN CALVIN BELIEVED, "FOR, such is the blindness with which we all rush into self-love that each one of us seems to himself to have just cause to be proud of himself and to despise all others in comparison." Calvin believed that the only remedy to this kind of self-love was self-denial, that is, a mindset that reminds us that all of our gifts are endowments of God's unmerited favor or grace. Furthermore, all and any gifts God chooses to bestow us were never intended for our own personal use or aggrandisement but were meant to edify the community of faith, the body of Christ. Calvin's statement on self-love would, no doubt, resonate with many people. Yet we must understand that Calvin was not advocating a posture that denigrated the self altogether, notwithstanding his view on total depravity! One need only read his opening remarks in his *Institutes of the Christian Religion*: "There is no deep knowing of God without a deep knowing of self and no deep knowing of self without a deep knowing of God."[1] Taking our cue from Calvin, the kind of attitude that takes pride in oneself and despises others must be exposed as being something other than authentic, wholesome self-love. To do so, we must examine the nature of self-love.

The Essence of Self-Love

Self plays a pivotal role in Christian spirituality and love of self is clearly espoused. A wholesome self-love in Christian spirituality is based upon the conviction that we are fearfully and wonderfully made.[2] This love recognizes that we are not an accident, but that God in his incredible grace cre-

1. Calvin, *Institutes of the Christian Religion*, 15.
2. Ps 139:14.

ated us on purpose and equipped us with talents and gifts that he intends us to use for the building up of the body of Christ.[3] A wholesome self-love liberates us to acknowledge and accept both our strengths and our liabilities, and allows us to be content to live and minister within the parameters they entail.

Self-love exceeds the realm of emotion to include our intellectual and existential gifts. In other words, not only how we *feel* about ourselves, but what we *think* about ourselves (perhaps self-esteem) and what we *do* for and to ourselves (self-care or self-abuse). I am going to suggest that authentic, wholesome self-love involves all three dimensions—affections, attitudes, and actions.

As Christ followers, we have also become what the apostle Paul calls the temple or dwelling place of the Holy Spirit,[4] and we are not our own but have been bought at a great price.[5] How sad to consider that many of us invest more time and energy into the care of our home or the church buildings than we do our own physical wellbeing. More will be said on this matter later.

Self-Love: A Basic Assumption

A wholesome self-love is an absolutely essential dimension of heart readiness for any leader. But it does not come easily to most of us. "Self-love does not come to us without effort. Defensiveness does. Self-protection does. The tendency to inflate ourselves like a puffer fish does. Love, self-love is an art and a craft. We achieve it, and get better at it, only with insight and practice."[6] Self-love, like any other love, involves risk.

It is very difficult to sustain the suggestion that Scripture presents self-love as a command. Even when Jesus describes second greatest commandments ("love your neighbour as yourself"), he does not present loving oneself as a command. Rather, Jesus assumes this to be a standard for the way in which the commandment to love our neighbor is to be lived out.

Some have cast self-love as "an inescapable problem for ethics,"[7] and for good reason. Ethics, whether secular, religious, or Christian, addresses

---

3. Rom 12:1–8; 1 Cor 12; Eph 4:11–13.
4. 1 Cor 3:16.
5. 1 Cor 6:20; 7:23.
6. Kent, *Falling in Love*, 7.
7. Weaver, *Self-Love*, 1.

our humanness and how we live in a world with others. Ethics basically, but perhaps oversimplified, addresses choices that have moral implications. The question of how one loves oneself rightly while loving one's neighbor at the same time has unnecessarily become a matter of moral choice for some people. It is even possible to posit that self-love and neighbor-love are antithetical.

With that said, I want to demonstrate in this chapter that it is not only possible to love oneself correctly without violating neighbor-love, it is essential to lovingly and effectively leading in ministry. Unfortunately, many have a difficult time getting past a myopic concept of self-love that equates it with selfishness, egoism, or a form of narcissism.[8]

Self-Love Versus Self-Centeredness

Although we can identify some apparent similarities between self-love and self-centeredness, these two concepts are diametrically opposed in essence. An example of self-centeredness, one that is markedly distinct from authentic self-love, is found in Jesus' parable of the Pharisee and Publican (Luke 18:9–14). Both went up to the temple to pray. But the Pharisee suffered from an intolerably inflated concept of his own morality, the result of a self-centered orientation. This self-absorbed mindset prevented the Pharisee from loving his neighbor (the Publican), and so saw the Publican primarily as someone who had failed to live up to the standard of his own Pharisaical righteousness.

It is difficult to deny the fact that self-love has the potential to drift toward unwholesome, even pathological self-centeredness. An excessive or imbalanced self-love that puts self before God and others is an aberration and, in fact, is idolatry and therefore sin. Such self-oriented affection does not liberate or equip a person for ministry to others. True love, according to the apostle Paul in 1 Corinthians 13:5, "is not self-seeking" (NIV) or "does not demand its own way" (Living Bible) for the simple reason it does not have to be! Self-centeredness of necessity must demand its own way even in the process of extending help to others. Self-centeredness is myopic and unable to see beyond oneself, whereas self-love is free to look outwardly.

Furthermore, self-centeredness is rooted in fear, and it causes a person to be profoundly insecure. Such people live life on a very short leash, and

8. Narcissism comes from the Greek myth of a handsome Greek youth who was doomed to fall in love with his own reflection in a pool of water.

they are fearful that venturing any distance from one's own interests is to invite disappointment and court failure. However, there is no merit to be gained through the maintenance of a chronic woe-is-me attitude. "A person who lives in constant awareness of failure and guilt probably is not going to be an effective spouse, parent, neighbor, or a fruitful Christian."[9] Nor, I would add, can such a person lead effectively. The remedy to such tendencies is not the purging of any semblance of self-love. Excessive self-love and self-hate are equally self-centered. Self-love is not to be *obliterated* by the cross. Rather, it is *redeemed* by the cross. Christ made it abundantly clear that the cross was to be a prominent daily feature in the life of anyone desiring to follow him.[10] How then does "death to self" reconcile with the self-love we have been considering?

Many of us as leaders are driven by a relentless, almost addictive need to legitimize our existence through the maintenance of outlandish schedules. Somehow or another we have convinced ourselves or been duped into believing that we are indispensable to God's kingdom work in our particular part of the world! This is a very real issue for many leaders, and I will address it later in this chapter.

Walter Trobisch argues that to love means to accept the object of that love as it really is.[11] That kind of love includes love of self. In fact, Trobisch suggests that love (acceptance) of oneself is foundational to any and all other kinds of love. I would argue that foundational to that kind of self-love is the love we considered in our first chapter: loving God with all we are.

Self-Love and Neighbor Love

Anytime the command to love one's neighbor appears in the New Testament it is without exception accompanied by the phrase "as yourself."[12] Furthermore, in the majority of these passages this double-edged command (loving God and loving our neighbor) is presented as the fulfillment of the entire law. But interpreting the phrase "as yourself" as a command exceeds the bounds of sound exegesis. As stated in the previous chapter on neighbor-love, the average person needs little or no urging to care for or preserve him or herself. Both Jesus and the apostle Paul assume that it

9. Brownback, *Danger of Self-Love*, 131.

10. Luke 9:23.

11. Trobisch, *Love Yourself*, 10.

12. Matt 22:39; Mark 12:31; Luke 10:27; Gal 5:14; Jas 2:8; Rom 13:9.

exists, because it is a built-in response. The problem is that, due to the fall, self-love has mutated either into inflated expressions of self-absorption or sunk into depleted expressions manifested in self-abuse or neglect.

As a child I was taught the acrostic JOY—Jesus first, Others second, and Yourself last. That is how one finds joy, I was told! The danger of prioritizing these relations in this manner is the potential of reading into Scripture what is not there. That is, we may be prone to think that we are to love our neighbor *instead* of ourselves. Rather than presenting a contrast or the antithesis of neighbor-love, self-love needs to be seen as the standard by which we assess our love for others. Recall that Jesus combines neighbor-love and self-love into an inseparable whole.

The image crafters of the marketing media have made it difficult for many people to maintain a proper concept of self-love and neighbor-love and a balanced tension between the two. When we allow ourselves to be exposed to the relentless barrage of images that are masterfully orchestrated by the advertising industry, a wholesome self-acceptance is likely to be undermined through the manipulative use of comparison and the subsequent creation of a malcontent. This condition then fosters self-centered entitlement and blurs wholesome self-love which, in turn, can taint our attitude toward our neighbor.

Yet, as we have already seen, Scripture assumes a place for self-love. In Ephesians 5, Paul weaves the concept of self-love into his teaching on marriage. Self-love stands out three times in this passage.[13] Loving your wife as your own self is not synonymous with egocentrism. In fact it is quite the opposite. Self-love is not a centripetal force that draws or sucks everything into the center of self. It is a centrifugal force that directs its energy outward, because the self is free and empowered to do so.

Self-Love and Self-Denial

How do we reconcile self-love with what Scripture teaches about self-denial? How does this concept of self-love coincide with those "self-denial" verses we find throughout Scripture? Did not Jesus teach us, "He who loves his own life loses it."?[14] And in Luke 14:26 what, then, did Jesus mean when he said, "If any one comes to me and does not hate . . . even his own life, he cannot be my disciple."? Furthermore, doesn't Paul warn young pas-

13. Eph 5: 28, 29, 31.
14. John 12:25.

tor Timothy that in the latter days there will be increased godlessness(as evidenced by a lengthy list that includes such things as people being greedy, proud, arrogant, abusive, disobedient to their parents, ungrateful, unholy, and lovers of themselves)?[15]

On the surface, self-love and self-denial may seem completely antithetical. In fact, through the centuries of Christian tradition some people have strongly contended that such realities cannot be reconciled; that is, we cannot love God with all we are while retaining any semblance of self-love. However, I have come to believe that self-love as well as self-denial are both legitimate and in fact mutually beneficial if understood in the light of God's Word. To begin with, self-denial does not assume or suggest self-neglect or abuse. What then does proper self-love look like when it is balanced with self-denial and clothed in our humanness? We can find no better window of understanding into this than what is found in the life and ministry of Jesus.

Jesus the Model of Self-Love

The selfless investment that Jesus made in the lives of his disciples and his sacrificial giving, ultimately in the laying down of his own life for the needs of others, remind us that self-love does not preclude costly sacrifice. But Jesus' ministry did not fizzle out as a result of reckless abandon and disregard for his own well-being. He recognized and embraced the limits of his humanness without guilt or shame. In addition, he maintained his love for the Father as the hub around which all other loves revolved, for it was that love that kept Jesus anchored in who he was and what he had come to do. It was because of a self-love rooted in a love for the Father that the writer to the Hebrews reminds us that Jesus "for the joy that was set before him, endured the cross, despising the shame and is seated at the right hand of the throne of God."[16] A life directed by a self-centered orientation would find no joy in a cross of any kind, nor would it possess the resources deep enough to endure the suffering and the shame associated with the cross.

At the outset of his ministry, when tested for forty days by Satan in the desert, Jesus' self-love was put to the test in the crucible of intense trial.[17] All three temptations specifically referred to in the gospel accounts were

15. 2 Tim 3:1–5.

16. Heb 12:2.

17. Mark 1:12.

fruitless efforts on Satan's part to persuade Jesus to operate from a position of misplaced self-love that was driven by concern for one's own needs and reputation.

What was it that enabled Jesus to give himself to and on the behalf of others—even before going to the cross? Just prior to the humiliating act of washing his disciples' feet, John makes this wonderful statement that provides a window into Jesus' own self-acceptance. In John 13:3–5 we read:

> Jesus knew that the Father had put all things under his power, and that he had come from God and was returning to God; so he got up from the meal, took off his outer clothing and wrapped a towel around his waist. After that, he poured water into a basin and began to wash his disciples' feet, drying them with the towel that was wrapped around him.

Paul explains further what was actually going on in that upper room. In Philippians 2 he reminds us of Christ's willingness to empty himself, forget about his reputation, and take on the role of a servant. Again this statement is preceded by an indication that Jesus was confident in who he truly was in essence, namely, equal with God. But self-acceptance did not foster the slightest degree of entitlement. Entitlement is necessary only when facing uncertainty or insecurity. As Walter Trobisch has so eloquently stated, "The obedience of self-denial presupposes the obedience of self-acceptance."[18]

Self-Love and Self-Acceptance

Self-preservation is an innate quality of humanness. We instinctively protect ourselves, physically, emotionally, and in every way without much instruction, so to speak. Such is not the case in terms of the self-love that we have been considering here. Most loves need to be learned and acted upon in order for them to develop. I did not love my wife the first time I met her. I was strongly attracted to her, but the love we now enjoy was planted, growing over time, and has continued to grow and deepen over the more than four decades we have known each other and the thirty-eight years we have been married. This was not a spontaneous or instantaneous love; it was a developmental love. However, the moment I laid eyes on each of our four children I experienced a spontaneous love. Despite the fact that none

---

18. Trobisch, *Love Yourself*, 19.

of them knew who I was, could not say my name, could do nothing but simply be, I would have laid down my life for each of them in a heartbeat.

There is a sense in which self-love is an acquired love that grows as our self-awareness develops. For many people, the first step toward self-awareness involves recognizing that self-love and self-acceptance are legitimate self-expressions that God intended to be part of humanness before the fall! One of the most devastating fallouts of the introduction of sin into the human experience has been the undermining of humanity's capacity for self-love. The first emotional response that Adam and Eve experienced following their intentional disregard for God's clear directive was shame, which in turn fostered the action of attempting to cover themselves. Self-love had become self-centeredness; self-awareness had become self-absorption. For the very first time there was something about their persons that they were driven to conceal, namely, their nakedness. But their nakedness was more than the mere embarrassing exposure of their physical bodies; it was much deeper. It was an emotional and spiritual vulnerability that was coupled with two unprecedented emotions—fear and shame. These emotions were completely absent prior to the entrance of sin.

I would venture to say that most of us experience a degree of discomfort upon receiving a compliment or praise. It is intriguing to me how vulnerable and exposed we can feel when someone is commending us or thanking us for a ministry well done. Often there seems to be a delicate blend of gratification from the knowledge that God has been pleased and gracious enough to use us in another person's life and a mild dose of embarrassment or awkwardness that comes from not really knowing what to say in response. We have allowed a flawed perception of humility to impinge on our thinking that, in turn, may force us to ward off or minimize any expression of praise or appreciation. So we fill the air with expressions like, "Well it wasn't me; it was all Him"; or "Glory to God, I'm just the instrument." Somehow we may think that it would be untenable to say, "Thank you, I appreciate you letting me know that. I'm humbled and grateful that you were blessed and God was honored." Yet, in the likelihood that we will be given compliments as ministry leaders, that self-love, and the consequent ability to receive and accept praise is so critical. A proper self-love allows us to receive an expression of thanks without it stroking or inflating our ego.

The other side of that coin, of course, is that in all likelihood we will also be on the receiving end of criticism that may or may not be constructive in nature. "[J]ustified criticism forces us to see ourselves differently, to incorporate new and unwelcome information into our understanding of who and what we are."[19] As a youth pastor in my first pastoral assignment, I was firmly confronted by my senior pastor for dropping the ball on a task he had asked me to complete. He was understandably upset and his criticism was justified. I was chagrined that the criticism was necessary in the first place. But as Sondra Wheeler stated so well, that new and unwelcome information gave me a new perspective on where I was in my development as a pastor. Because my senior pastor had made it abundantly clear that he loved me and had every confidence in me prior to the confrontation, my self-love was actually strengthened while my self-centeredness was brought down a notch or two. Wholesome self-love is not enhanced through the avoidance of criticism, but self-centeredness likely will be. Put another way, wholesome self-love places us in the position of being able to receive either commendation or criticism in a manner that will nudge us closer to Christ and ultimately bring him glory.

Some would suggest that there is a dimension that must precede the ability to love either ourselves or others, namely the ability to allow ourselves to be loved. As 1 John 4:19 says, "We love him because he first loved us." Others, however, believe it is the other way around; that is, before we can accept love from anyone else, including God, we must first learn to love ourselves. I am inclined to believe that accepting God's love for us has the power to short circuit the influence of past circumstances or other people's actions (or lack thereof) from robbing us of the capacity to love ourselves. In other words, possessing the knowledge that God's love for us defies comprehension and, as a result, watching our love for him grow is the soil of truth in which our self-love must germinate.

Dr. Theodor Bovet expressed it this way: "If I love myself in the right way, then it is impossible for me to remain standing still. On the contrary, I want to change so that I can become that which God desires me to become. In the same way we should love also our neighbor."[20] Acceptance does not imply the condoning of behavior that is harmful or that puts oneself or others at risk. The reason God accepts us, and has predestined us,[21] is so that we can be conformed to the likeness of his son. What this means, then, is that self-acceptance is far removed from a resignation that merely thinks, "Well, I just have to accept the fact that this is just who I am." Self-

19. Wheeler, *What We Were Made For*, 49.
20. Cited in Trobisch, *Love Yourself*, 27.
21. Rom 8:28–29.

acceptance needs to be nurtured in the knowledge that God desires us to become more and more like his son, the Lord Jesus.

Loving Our Self Holistically

Love for oneself must be personally holistic, encompassing one's whole person—body, soul, and spirit. The apparent disregard that many of us seem to display toward our physical well-being makes me wonder if we have not been influenced by a quasi-Gnostic mindset that considers the body inconsequential at best or, worse, an encumbrance or even sinful at worst. Historically, Christians in the Global North have tended to dichotomize our humanness into the physical/visible and the spiritual/invisible, and in doing so have constructed a hierarchical ranking of the spiritual over the physical. Speaking of the therapeutic value of dance or other forms of bodily self-expression, Paul Tournier states: "It is not a matter of accepting willy-nilly that one has a body, but of rediscovering its value, of using it as a genuine manifestation of one's person and becoming aware once more of *its spiritual significance*."[22]

It's the Only Body You Get!

Dietrich Bonhoeffer reminds us so clearly how important our bodies are: "Man was created a body, the Son of God appeared on earth in the body, he was raised in the body, in the sacrament the believer receives the Lord Christ in the body, and the resurrection of the deal will bring about the perfected fellowship of God's spiritual-physical creatures."[23] The apostle Paul was a man who knew what it was like to be challenged physically, and yet he came to the point of accepting his own physical frailty. In his second letter to the Corinthian church he made the following statement: "So we do not lose heart. Though our outer self is wasting away, our inner self is being renewed day by day."[24] His response to his physical body was not a resignation of despair but a realization of hope. What Paul's confidence in his daily inner renewal does *not* do is provide room to neglect our physical well-being because it is "wasting away" anyway. Relatively few of us would

22. Tournier, *Place for You*, 67. Emphasis added.

23. Bonhoeffer, *Life Together*, 19–20.

24. 2 Cor 4:16.

say we are thoroughly comfortable or satisfied with our physical body. I suspect that the vast majority of us, if given the opportunity, would identify without hesitation at least one aspect of our physique that we would like to change or get rid of altogether. This should come as no surprise really: we are immersed in a culture that worships the body and has deified physical beauty as the epitome of personal value and worth. While succumbing to such flawed influences we do our best to compensate, if not cover up altogether, our perceived physical flaws. Is this not reminiscent of Adam and Eve's initial response to their nakedness? The exercise of spiritual disciplines that neglect or marginalize physical discipline does not reflect a scriptural perspective. Paul reminds Timothy, "For physical training is of some value [notice he does not say, "is of *no* value."], but godliness has value for all things, holding promise for both the present life and the life to come."[25]

The kind of self-love essential to effectiveness in ministry leadership pays attention to one's physical well-being without becoming obsessed with or idolizing the body. When it comes to the physical dimension of our person, studies among pastors would seem to indicate that more often than not our problem is one of neglect, not obsession.

There are very few vocations that are more physically, emotionally, and spiritually demanding than leadership in a ministry context. Researchers have concluded recently that the act of preaching a single thirty-five to forty minute sermon is as physically and emotionally taxing as an average eight-hour work day in an office. Those ministry leaders who are required to preach two, three, or more times any given weekend are asking their bodies to cram two or three days of work into one. That itself should be motivation enough for a ministry leader to take care of his or her physical well-being. Furthermore, Paul admonishes his readers to be mindful of the fact that our bodies are the temple of the Holy Spirit: we are not our own but have been bought with a price. Therefore we are to *glorify God in our body*.[26] Clearly one of the ways in which we do this is by preserving our bodies from immorality.[27] But should we not also glorify God by caring for the body God has entrusted to us?

If we as leaders are not exercising appropriate self-love through proper rest, diet, and exercise (I know this is so basic), then how dare we challenge

25. 1 Tim 4:8.

26. 1 Cor 6:19–20 (emphasis added).

27. 1 Cor 6:15–18.

those we are leading to present their bodies as living sacrifices, wholly and acceptable to God![28] I have had too many disconcerting conversations with colleagues in ministry leadership that indicate we are flippant about our health. Indeed, we are almost proud of our overeating and lack of adequate rest and exercise, or we seem to accept such habits simply as occupational hazards of leadership in ministry. There is nothing commendable or glorifying to God about burning out prematurely by neglecting the body God has provided us for our use and his glory. More will be said on this below when we consider Sabbath rest and self-love.

Self-Love and Our Emotional Pulse

I have to wonder if the unnecessary and untimely departure of many from leadership positions in ministry is not precipitated by their inability or unwillingness to love him or herself, and a fear of failure that is compounded by the fruitless tendency to compare him or herself with others. Leaders often feel a chronic absence of affirmation, or even minimal tangible evidence, that they are making a significant contribution to people's lives. That sense of futility, coupled with the demands of kingdom work, understandably can bring ministry leaders to a point of serious questioning of their personal worth, thus inhibiting self-love and self-acceptance. Such feelings have also caused some ministry leaders to question the validity of their call to ministry leadership. Jesus promised that in this world we would experience the suffocating angst of tribulation (John 16:33). Investment in the work of the kingdom often goes without affirmation, but Jesus' promise that tribulation will come is seamlessly linked to that unshakable assurance that he has overcome the world. His overcoming the world has not circumvented the possibility, indeed the likelihood, of tribulation. But tribulation is incapable of robbing us of good cheer if we are willing to rest in *his* overcoming.

Reflecting on his own experience during the Second World War, Walter Trobisch commented, "Faith did not free me from fear, but fear forced me to believe."[29] We are not called to deny or suppress fear. It is possible to "take heart" or "be of good cheer" (KJV) even in the midst of tribulation for the simple reason that though Jesus did not promise to overcome our fear, he did promise to overcome the source of our fears—the world.

28. Rom 12:1–2.

29. Trobisch, *Love Yourself*, 36.

Healthy authentic self-love requires accurate self-awareness. Sometimes that self-knowledge is more than we want to know. How does one acquire this kind of authentic self-knowledge? It is critical we begin with the perspective of our creator himself as revealed in his word.

There is danger in making the term *self-love* a synonym for self-fulfillment, self-happiness, self-gratification, self-centeredness, or a host of other "self-isms." The distinction between self-love and these other loves often has been blurred through such influences as the masterful manipulation of marketing media. And honestly, how is this confused state of self-love working for us? Divorce rates are higher than at any other time; we spend more time at work and less with our families; we eat poorly, exercise infrequently. Despite all best efforts, the rate of domestic violence against women remains stubbornly high and the disparity in wages between equally qualified men and women is shameful.

Loving ourselves properly frees us to accept and celebrate that we are "fearfully and wonderfully made," and that as God's own creation we bear his very image. When Paul spoke of "beating his body" and keeping it under subjection[30] he was not advocating self-hatred or self-abuse. Nor was he implying any inherent evil or sin associated with our corporeal being. Rather, he is talking of a refusal to allow his physical self to dominate his life. He did not engage in extreme ascetic practices of self-denial; rather, he reminds us that we, as believers, are God's temple and that the Spirit lives in us. Lest his readers miss the significance of what is being said, he underscores it by saying, "If anyone destroys God's temple, God will destroy him; for God's temple is sacred and you are that temple."[31]

I recognize that the pronouns Paul uses in this passage are in the plural, that is, when saying "you are that temple," he is saying you in the plural, you corporately. Therefore, it could be argued that Paul is inferring that the Spirit resides in our fellowship, or that the sacred temple of God referenced here is the gathering of the saints, and not specifically our physical bodies. However, as we saw earlier in Paul's admonition in 1 Corinthians 6:19, "your body is a temple of the Holy Spirit within you, whom you have from God."

As legitimate and important as it is, self-love has the potential, if allowed, to distort all other loves, including our love for our neighbor and our love for God. When self-love becomes so self-absorbed that it places self at

30. 1 Cor 9:27.
31. 1 Cor 3:16–18.

the center of the universe, all other loves will be attenuated accordingly. Loving others can and should bring us pleasure. But when that pleasure or self-gratification becomes the driving force behind loving others, then distortion and ultimately disappointment inevitably follows. For example, just as a parent experiences joy in meeting the needs of their newborn child, as demanding and inconvenient as it may be, those of us who serve others in ministry can enjoy the sense of being needed and appreciated. In many scenarios such as mate/mate, parent/child, and leader/follower, care for others and efforts to meet others' needs can easily devolve into a manipulative desire for power and control or personal satisfaction.

Authentic self-love allows us to love others without possessing or owning them and is willing at the appropriate time to release those we love. The "leaving-cleaving-one flesh" rhythm of Genesis 2:24–25 is contingent on wholesome self-love. That is not to suggest that the releasing and departure of loved-ones are easy and natural. They are not. Sondra Wheeler says it well: "Love *is* hard and we do not always get it right. Nature is in need of grace."[32] The reason we need or desire the love of others is not the result of the fall or a distortion caused by an aberrant self-love. That desire is rather a reflection of God's love, both in terms of self-love within the Trinity and love for the other, namely his entire creation. Self-love needs relationship to flourish. Likewise, relationship needs self-love to flourish. As Dietrich Bonhoeffer says:

> Let him who cannot be alone beware of community . . . Let him who is not in community beware of being alone . . . Each by itself has profound perils and pitfalls. One who wants fellowship without solitude plunges into the void of words and feelings, and the one who seeks solitude without fellowship perishes in the abyss of vanity, self-infatuation, and despair.[33]

So many of our own personal struggles are rooted in our perception of self-love and our efforts to maintain a balance between self-love and other loves. Emotional conflicts can arise between a sense of obligation (what we should do) and personal desires (what we want to do). From a Christian perspective, should obligation to the other always trump personal desires or needs? How do obligation and commitment weigh out in the scale of scriptural discernment in relation to personal need and self-love?

32. Wheeler, *What We Were Made For*, 104.
33. Bonhoeffer, *Life Together*, 77.

A flawed perception of self-love that floats adrift from scriptural moorings can lead in one of two radically opposed yet equally devastating directions. One turns inward in a self-absorbed direction that generates an attitude of entitlement or self-preservation that minimizes or neglects altogether love for others. By contrast, the other direction turns outward, driven by an inordinate sense of obligation that minimizes or neglects altogether appropriate attention and care for oneself. Walter Trobisch warns of the potential danger of entering into helping ministries for the wrong reason. "The choice of entering into people-oriented professions may be motivated by the need to be needed."[34]

I would argue that the first direction, the one that places self at the center, dominates in human culture. By contrast, self-sacrifice is the rare and wonderful exception, not the norm. I am very grateful for the privilege of living in a country that affords me an enviable standard of living and an amazing and generous world of opportunity and freedom. On April 17, 1982, Queen Elizabeth II signed into Canadian law the Constitution Act, 1982. The first part of this act is what is known as the Canadian Charter of Rights and Freedoms, which enshrined into the constitutional apparatus of the country certain political rights for Canadian citizens and civil rights for all residing in Canada. Many would see this as the necessary continuation and development of the declaration adopted by the United Nations General Assembly in December of 1948, known as the Universal Declaration of Human Rights. Who can fault any effort or declaration that is motivated by a commitment to the preservation of certain rights to which all humans are inherently entitled? The challenge for upholding such rights is two-fold: first, fallen humanity's tendency is toward an inward self-preservation that secondly, is exacerbated by a declaration that is top-heavy in rights but rather light on the responsibilities of Canadian citizens.

The momentum of efforts to curtail inhumane atrocities witnessed around the globe (for example, one group deems another unworthy of rights or life itself), has swung way out to the other end of the spectrum where we as individuals, now reinforced by charters of right and freedoms, now assess circumstances primarily through the matrix of our own personal entitlements. This is not the self-love of Scripture.

As mentioned above, the remedy to the dilemma of misplaced or distorted self-love is not its eradication, but its redemption. We are not called to suppress self-love in the hope that it will eventually fade into

---

34. Trobisch, *Love Yourself*, 29.

non-existence. Rather, like every other dimension in our lives, we are to live out our self-love from the cross, being ever mindful and able to say, "I have been crucified with Christ. It is no longer I who live, but Christ who lives in me. And the life I now live in the flesh I live by faith in the Son of God, who loved me and gave himself for me."[35] Living our lives in this way will remind us that, ironically and paradoxically, authentic self-love in the life of the Christ follower is not about *us* ultimately. It is simply another vehicle through which we can demonstrate our wholehearted love for the Lord.

In other words our love for ourselves must be a reflection of our love for the Lord. We are to love the Lord holistically not selectively, that is with our entire person. How do we love ourselves holistically? Is it possible for us to be both the object and the subject of our self-love? Doing so involves embracing who God has made us to be—our abilities and liabilities; strengths and limitations—without shame or regret. But keeping that in proper perspective requires that we avoid the kind of positive self-talk that places self at the center of the universe and gratefully acknowledging that, as Paul said, by the grace of God I am what I am.[36] My identity, my purpose, my abilities, my future—all there is about me is by the grace of God.

Self-Love and the Imago Dei

Understanding the true nature and importance of self-love is best arrived at through bringing the triune nature of God to bear on our humanity. The image of God that has been invested in us as God's creation is communal in nature. What does this mean with respect to our consideration of self-love? Simply this, self-love is not expressed or experienced solely in isolation individually, but in relation communally. As Bonhoeffer's comment (cited earlier) reminds us, community and the individual are not antithetical. Rather they are symbiotic. Or at least they should be. However, one cannot deny the potential for negative impact that community can have on an individual. Social psychologists have demonstrated how an individual's beliefs about and attitudes towards oneself develop on the basis of his or her interpretations of the attitudes and beliefs of others.[37]

There is no question that such is the case for the vast majority of us, and particularly those who find themselves in leadership and ministry

35. Gal 2:20.

36. 1 Cor 15:9–11.

37. See Grenz, *Social God*, 310.

roles. The dichotomy between being a task-oriented and relationally oriented person can foster a tendency among some to see themselves as being immune to any communal imprint on their self-perception. I would argue that many, if not the majority, of us are quite susceptible to the response of those we lead and the impact these responses have on our self-love. The proverbial rugged individual who apparently manages to minimize the influence of public opinion through the effective development of the required "thick skin" is a rarity, if not an anomaly. We do not develop a wholesome self-love by insulating ourselves from what others think about us, nor, on the other hand, by swinging out to the other end of the spectrum and allowing ourselves to fall victim to the tyrannical influence of others' opinions. Biblically based self-awareness in the context of community provides the necessary infrastructure for wholesome and legitimate self-love. The domination of individual autonomy, the birth child of the Enlightenment, is losing or already has lost currency in the post-modern ethos. More important, it is a life posture that could never be sustained by Scripture. All of this serves to underscore that biblical self-love is not to be confused with humanistic individualism, nor with many of the other tantalizing self-isms offered within our culture today.

The importance of seeing self-love in the context of community, in relation with others, however, is incomplete in the absence of seeing the individual and community in relation to the triune God.[38] We cannot love ourselves by ourselves! The greatest commandment according to Jesus is to love God and our neighbor as ourselves. All three dimensions are included with self-love properly positioned in relation to love of God and love of neighbor. The relation between these three loves is not linear or sequential. Rather, it is more like what some of the early church Fathers used as they attempted to convey the relationship with the Trinity. The term they used was *perichoresis*, a dancing or walking around. John of Damascus, for instance, described it as a "cleaving together." Even when Jesus called his apostles (Mark 3:13–19) he called them into community, not solitude. "He appointed twelve—designating them apostles—that they might be with him . . ."

The challenge we must confront in our thinking as Christians is how to balance or reconcile a love for ourselves with an awareness of our sinfulness and subsequent unworthiness before God. It is very easy to

38. Ibid., 312.

find ourselves on the see-saw of thinking, "I'm wonderful/I'm sinful; I'm lovable/I'm unlovely."

Self-Love and Self-Identity

Self-love assumes a certain depth of self-awareness, or what social scientists refer to as identity development. Theories that address the development of self-identity are numerous and cover a wide array of imaginative possibilities. A theory that is germane to our discussion here is reflected in what some have called a dramaturgical model. Based on a drama motif of theatrical performance, a person is seen as an actor following scripts and taking on ever-changing roles.[39] Sometimes the scripts we are expected to read or the roles we are expected to fulfill are more reflective of the culture we have been invited to join or a predecessor we are following. Whether we are stepping into a lead or associate role, rightly or wrongly, for good or ill, comparison is inevitable. It is during such liminal stages of transition that vulnerability is often most keenly felt. Biblical self-love has the capacity to enable us not only to navigate the scary white water of transition but to learn from and be strengthened by it.

For five years I had the joy of working with a dear friend in team-teaching a course entitled "Leadership and group dynamics in stress." Our classroom was located in the bush of northern Saskatchewan for approximately ten days in February. Snow was commonly above our knees and daytime temperatures hovered around minus twenty degrees centigrade (four below zero Fahrenheit). The content of the course included critical input on winter survival in the bush and leadership principles from the life of Jesus, which my friend George taught effectively. But perhaps the most critical, and for some students the most challenging, material presented in the course was on orienteering—how to use a compass and topographical map and how to read the lay of the land.

After approximately five or six days of intensive instruction, the students' grasp of survival techniques and orienteering skills were put to the test. Students were dropped off at different starting points in the groups to which they had been assigned. Equipped with three compasses to compensate for any variances that might occur, one map for the group, and one backpack each with enough food, water, and winter survival gear that they were responsible to pack (that is, if they listened during instruction

39. See Grenz, *Social God*, 311–12.

times!), they were given approximately twelve hours to reach their preassigned destination.

Students quickly learned how critical it was for them to know—beyond any shadow of a doubt—where they started from and where they needed to be. They also absolutely had to believe the readings on their compass and trust their maps. And so they did. One finds a similar challenge navigating through the landscape of self-identity and self-love.

The problem with the approaches of many highly influential theorists, such as Erich Fromm and Carl Rogers, is that they began from a humanistic orientation with us as humans. Self-love that is rooted in the shallow soil of humanity divorced from the creator God has influenced the historical upsurge of interest in what has become known as the self-help movement. Rogers' approach to counseling, for instance, avoided all intrusive directives such as "you should or should not" and served instead to guide the person to what already existed in themselves. This was based on his conviction that "the individual possess a 'self-actualizing' tendency, something like a homing device that directs us so that intuitively we know the path that will lead us to self-actualization or fulfillment."[40] The problem, of course, is that other people and influences have the capacity to override this internal guidance system that every human apparently possesses.

The strongest influences in disrupting a person's internal self-actualizing capability are typically the significant others in a person's life. Therefore, the role of the counselor is to develop a relationship with the client in which the counselor is established as a significant other who then communicates unconditional acceptance of the client. Rogers believed that when people are convinced that they are unconditionally accepted and loved, then and only then are they capable of accepting and loving themselves. Underlying this theory is the element of entitlement: all people by virtue of their humanness are entitled to unconditional acceptance. Performance standards of any sort are deemed unnecessary. Self-love, according to this system of thought, is not selfishness. Rather it is a prerequisite to self-fulfillment or self-actualization which, in turn, is necessary for any person to make a meaningful contribution to society at large.

---

40. Brownback, *Danger of Self-Love*, 80.

Self-Love and the Cross

A dangerous spinoff of an approach like Rogers' is the development of a mindset that sees self-love as the panacea to all of our personal woes. We are encouraged to love ourselves on the basis that God himself has loved us, and he is willing to accept us unconditionally, just as we are. The problem with this, when taken to the extreme, is the inadvertent or intentional avoidance of a part of our humanness that God cannot and will not accept, namely our sin.

An approach to self-love that is anthropocentric, that is, an approach that begins with humanity somehow, has taken the truth of our being made in the image of God and drifted into a mindset that virtually sets the image of God up as a human accomplishment or as something that we have achieved rather than received. Scripturally we begin, not with the one who bears the image of God (*ourselves*), but with God whose image we bear. In John 15:5, Jesus makes it very clear that even though we bear the image of God, apart from Christ we are capable of absolutely nothing! There is no room for an autonomous independence from Christ. To begin with humanity in setting the course for our understanding of self-love is to invest humanity with an autonomy that belongs rightly and solely to God.

Often our desperate attempts to cling tenaciously to some sense of self-worth are fueled by an understanding of redemption that rather boldly suggests that God would not sacrifice his own son for creatures who are of no value or worth.[41] Osborne puts it this way: "There must be something truly wonderful about us if he (God) can love and accept us so readily."[42] Statements such as this, however, miss the whole point of redemption and undermine the wonder of God's grace. God's grace has been extended for reasons completely beyond and separate from humanity's worth. Redemption has nothing to say about our value or worth; it has everything to say about the depth of God's unfathomable grace.

Self-love that allows us to understand and appreciate our worth does not begin with introspection, by looking inwardly. Rather, it begins with adoration, looking upward to God who not only created us in his image, but loved us and gave himself for us. *Authentic and effective self-love begins at and is sustained by the cross.* If our self-love is dependent upon the affirmation of others or the success of our own efforts, then we are building

---

41. See Hoekema *Christian Looks at Himself*, 22.

42. Osborne, *Art of Learning to Love Yourself*, 137.

on the shifting sands that, at best, are unpredictable and unstable. Although this is not the private reserve of those of us in leadership or ministry positions, I would we argue that such persons are the most prone to this kind of struggle.

I am not, however, advocating a perspective that sees humanity as being completely valueless or useless. We are God's workmanship, created according to his intelligent and masterful design; we do possess abilities and good gifts. But as James 1:17 reminds us, "Every good gift and every perfect gift is from above, coming down from the Father of lights with whom there is no variation or shadow due to change." Jesus uses the illustration of the vine and the branches to explain what this looks like in the life of any individual.[43] It is not the branches per se that produce fruit. They simply bear the fruit that the vine produces. A branch can only bear fruit when it is grafted into the vine. Thus, the significance of Jesus' statement is that apart from him we can do nothing.

This dependence upon the Lord is not a flaw in our humanness. Paul was able to glory in it, saying: "But he said to me, 'My grace is sufficient for you, for my power is made perfect in weakness.' Therefore I will boast all the more gladly of my weaknesses, so that the power of Christ may rest upon me."[44] Self-love is not synonymous with feeling good about ourselves, nor is it contingent on being convinced that we can do it, whatever "it" may be. Self-love is rooted in a different kind of confidence, the kind Paul also spoke of: "Such is the confidence that we have through Christ toward God. Not that we are sufficient in ourselves to claim anything as coming from us, but our sufficiency is from God, who made us competent to be ministers of the a new covenant."[45]

Self-Love and Self-Confidence

Unfortunately, self-love has been likened to, if not equated with, self-confidence. Invariably self-confidence falls prey to self-comparison through which we can always find someone better or worse than us. Had the boy David gone out to face his Goliath bolstered by some lathered up self-confidence, chanting "You can do this, David, you can do this," or had he succumbed to Saul's weakness of taking stock of his our resources and

43. John 15.
44. 2 Cor 12:9.
45. 2 Cor 3:4–6.

comparing them to those of the giant, there would have been no victory for Israel that day. David had not succumbed to some wild fantasies. He was possessed by a major dose of realism. He was fully aware of what he was up against. But, just as critically, he was not weakened by a grandiose perception of his own resources or by the enormity of his enemy's arsenal and ability by comparison. Instead, his strength came from God. Thus he could say to Goliath, "You come to me with a sword and with a spear and with a javelin . . . But I come to you in the name of the Lord of hosts, the God of the armies of Israel, whom you have defied. This day the Lord will deliver you into my hands . . ."[46] Authentic self-love does not harbor unrealistic hopes and expectations regarding our own abilities nor does it wallow in our apparent liabilities.

Self-Love and Sabbath Rest

I know of very few concepts that have caused more confusion, and ultimately disregard, than the scriptural principle of Sabbath rest. For many the idea of Sabbath rest resides in the Old Testament under the rubric of Mosaic law and therefore has little or no significance for Christ followers today. On the other hand, many others including those who live according to the Orthodox Jewish faith and Seventh Day Adventists, embrace the Sabbath, specifically Saturday, as eminently important. I am prepared to argue that engaging in the kind of wholesome self-love that is essential to effectiveness in ministry leadership is quite impossible in the absence of a biblical understanding and consistent practice of Sabbath rest.

For many, the concept of Sabbath rest has been fostered in a conservative Christian environment in which Sundays in particular were characterised by major limitations. In such a tradition, not only did we not work (unless, of course, you were a pastor!), we tried to avoid making others work. This was the tradition that I grew up in. Thus, we would not go to restaurants on the Sabbath because that would create the need for someone to work. Interestingly enough, that did not exclude my mom from having to prepare, serve, and clean up the Sunday roast, the biggest meal of the week! Furthermore, not only were we not to work on the Sabbath, we were not to play. We were to rest, but again, within limits. It is little surprise then that Sundays became my least favorite day of the week. I had missed the whole point of what Jesus said regarding Sabbath: "The Sabbath was made

46. 1 Sam 17:45–46.

for man, not man for the Sabbath. So the Son of Man is lord even of the Sabbath."[47]

Let me stress at this point how grateful I am to my parents who, despite the slight imbalance on the "don't" aspect of Sunday, did teach me well that in God's economy the rhythm of six days work, one day rest, was a principle that was intended for our good and for his glory. The avoidance or neglect of a sabbatical rhythm in our lives is one of the most unloving acts we can commit against ourselves. The biggest challenge for many of us is in removing Sabbath rest from the realm of the "have to" into the realm of the "get to." As G. K. Chesterton wrote, "It is the healthy man who does the useless things; the sick man is not strong enough to be idle."[48]

I have no intention of duplicating some of the excellent works that have been written on this subject.[49] But a few comments will hopefully assist in gaining appreciation for the reason why Sabbath rest and self-love are organically linked.

When we look at the first time the word Sabbath appears in Scripture, namely the creation narrative in Genesis 1, we discover with some help from those who know the Hebrew language that the words *Sabbath*, *seven*, and *rest* all share the same root, which in Hebrew is *Shabbat*. The essence of this root is to cease, desist, or rest. It connotes the idea of completion or of being interrupted. Thus, when we read that on the seventh day God rested from his creative activity, it was not because creating a universe took a pile of energy and God was in need of recuperating! God rested for one reason—he was finished! The Sabbath was the seventh day for God, coming at the end of his creative work. But note this, for humanity, it was the first day. Sabbath rest for us as humans is not something that we earn so that we can enjoy the weekend. It is to be the first day that orients the rest of our week.

God did two things with that seventh day: he blessed it and declared it holy.[50] This was to be a day set apart from the rest, a day of blessing. And all this was done prior to the entrance of sin and the fall of humanity. However, let us remember that the Sabbath was not introduced on Mount Sinai when

47. See the whole paragraph, Mark 2:23–28.

48. Chesterton, *Orthodoxy*, 14.

49. Three of the best works on Sabbath I have read are Buchanan: *The Rest of God: Restoring Your Soul by Restoring Your Sabbath*; Dawn: *The Sense of Call: A Sabbath Way of Life for Those Who Serve God, the Church and the World*; and Herschel: *The Sabbath: Its Meaning for Modern Man*.

50. Gen 2:3.

God gave the law. When we look at the way the Sabbath is referenced in the Decalogue (Ten Commandments), we learn something significant.

In Deuteronomy 5:12–15 we find further emphasis on the people's identity and the role Sabbath was to play in reminding them of this role:

> Observe the Sabbath day, to keep it holy, as the Lord your God commanded you. Six days you shall labor and do all your work, but the seventh day is a Sabbath to the Lord your God. On it you shall not do any work, you or your son or your daughter or your male servant or your female servant, or your ox or your donkey or any of your livestock, or the sojourner who is within your gates, that your male servant and your female servant may rest as well as you. You shall remember that you were a slave in the land of Egypt, and the Lord your God brought you out from there, with a mighty and an outstretched arm. Therefore the Lord your God commanded you to keep the Sabbath day.

This was to be a day to remind Israel where God had brought them; to remind them of their relationship with God. Taking one day in seven as a blessed, holy day was to be a birthmark, as it were, that distinguished Israel from all the surrounding nations.

Turning our thoughts to the New Testament, and in particular to the life and ministry of Jesus, we are confronted with more evidence that Sabbath rest was to have a significant role in the lives of his followers. Probably more than any other aspect of Jesus' ministry, the one that irritated the religious people of his day as much or more than any was his perceived violation of Sabbath laws. One of the strongest examples is found in John's gospel.[51] We learn that the religious leaders were agitated to the point of questioning his authority as one from God because he did not keep the Sabbath. Even bringing life and healing into people's lives on the Sabbath got Jesus onto the death list of the religious leaders of his day.[52]

For that reason many people have come to the unfortunate conclusion that Jesus did away with the Sabbath, and that all the significance attached to it in Judaistic thinking was transcended by what Jesus did. It was not that Jesus did not honor the Sabbath, it was that he chose to do so in a way that differed significantly from the religious leaders of the day. Let us remember that these leaders established a Sabbath fraught with obligation

---

51. John 9:16.

52. Mark 3:1–6.

and limitation. Jesus' actions and teachings take it an entirely differently direction, presenting the Sabbath as a *gift* from God to humanity.

Rather than restricting our activity, Sabbath was to provide opportunity for refreshment and worship. But we must understand Jesus is *not* saying, therefore, that it doesn't matter what you do on the Sabbath or that you can do what you want. Instead he affirms and underscores the very purpose of Sabbath: to bring wholeness, to bring physical refreshment and spiritual renewal.

Having reminded ourselves of the significance of Sabbath rest in light of creation, the law and life and ministry of Jesus, it is hard to dispute the fact that Sabbath rest was never intended by God to be a punishment or restriction, nor was it intended to be an option. Sabbath rest is not an elective; it is part of the core curriculum. It is not something to be engaged because we have to or ought to. Rather it is to be because we get to. Let me put it this way, *Sabbath rest is both a gift that reflects God's grace and a command that reflects his holiness.*

Here is where I think we have strayed to various degrees: We have encumbered our Sabbath with the limitations and restrictions that were essential in the covenantal relation between God and Israel, although even here we are so selective. In addition, we have completely ignored the Sabbath and in so doing have transformed it into meaninglessness on the misguided notion that it is solely associated with Old Testament law and is therefore unnecessary or unimportant through the grace of God in Christ. The intriguing thing to me is that the fourth commandment is the only one that we treat this way. We would never think of casting any of the other nine commandments in the same light! Finally, we have marginalized the Sabbath to the extent that it has become little or nothing more than the proverbial day off, stripped of anything sacred or holy. Quite frankly, this last point concerns me the most because it hints at the fact that we are in danger of losing a sense of the sacred, and what God's holiness means in our lives and how the holiness of God will be reflected in our use of time.

Our refusal to observe Sabbath rest on a consistent basis belies an attitude that suggests we are indispensable to the efficient management of the universe—or at least our ministries! By working well and hard during our work-a-day world we affirm the reality that God has gifted us and called us to do something; it affirms that for whatever reason, God has chosen to use us (amazing!) and that someday we will give an account of what we have done. In other words, our work declares that we do have a part to play in what God is doing in the world—be that in the office, the classroom, the lab, or the worksite. But by taking a complete break (one in seven), we remind ourselves that who we are first and foremost is not tied to what we *do*. We are first and foremost beloved children of God. Furthermore, we are declaring to others and perhaps more importantly to ourselves, that in the grand scheme of things we are *not* indispensable. God really does not need us, yet we are greatly loved by him.

Sabbath allows us to stop, having no agenda and not feeling guilty. Why? So we can take inventory of the extent to which the activities we engage in (activities that consume our time, energy, and money) feed our egos, but starve our souls.[53]

I am well aware that there needs to be a strong element of balance in this matter of Sabbath rest. I have had pastors share with me how frustrating it has been to hire a young and aspiring ministry leader whose life seems to be top heavy in Sabbath rest! Though admittedly difficult at times to maintain, the balance between authentic Sabbath rest and a strong work ethic is essential to effectiveness in ministry leadership.

Well you may say, "Bill, this sounds so idyllic and wonderful, but you have no idea what it's like in my world. I can't afford a whole day off each week, or thereabouts." To such a response I would say, "You're right. I don't know what it's like. I can only imagine. I have numerous friends who make their living in the corporate world. I know people in the military and police services who face challenges I never will. But I have to say this, in the grand scheme of life, friend, as a Christ follower, you can't afford not to take time for Sabbath rest. That is just how our creator God has hardwired us."

The challenge, of course, is what should Sabbath rest look like then in our harried, frenetic age of grace in which we live? Ah—here's where Scripture is quieter than some of us would like. There is very little in the New Testament that provides an agenda for the day, and for good reason. A day of Sabbath rest is perhaps the only one that should have no agenda! The reality is that those who have young children at home will likely consider Sabbath rest in a slightly different manner than those who don't. We go through seasons of life through which the structure and even the timing of Sabbath rest will vary. Sabbath rest needs to be consistent by its *presence* but not necessarily by its *praxis*. The essence of Sabbath rest is not linked to one particular day of the week; it is tied to the posture of your heart. Being Christlike means knowing when and how to work and when and how to

---

53. Buchanan, *Rest of God*, 48.

stop. "To fail to see the value of simply being with God and doing nothing is to miss the heart of Christianity." We struggle with this in part because we live in a culture that embraces values such as "time is money" or "time is of the essence." Overcoming this struggle is as simple as saying, "*No.*" Time is God's.

What Does It Look Like, Practically?

I grew up with a concept of the Sabbath that was basically a day of "don't." I knew what I could not do, which seemed to include most things I enjoyed. It was to be a day of rest, in which we disengaged from the normal responsibilities of work and the world. If this is to be a day of rest, what are some of the activities from which we need rest? How about some of the following:

1. Rest from consumerism: Set aside this one day for not buying anything—not because you have to, but because you get to.

2. Rest from worry: Easier said than done, I realize. It takes faith and practice. It is a day to focus on God's sovereign care for us and all that concerns us in an unhurried and unharried way.

3. Rest for/in creation: Take your kids or go by yourself to a place where you can be surrounded by God's creation.

4. Rest from work: Make this one day that has no "to do" list. As one whose ministry involves mental and oral activities, one of the best ways I can rest from my type of work is to engage in some kind of manual activity. I happen to enjoy woodworking and dabble occasionally in acrylic and oil painting. I also enjoy playing my guitar. Engaging in creative activities that call for the development of skills that are normally shelved on regular days of work and ministry provides a wonderful, re-creative Sabbath.

5. Rest from social networking: Try disengaging from the world of cyberspace and cell phones! The world will survive famously without you. The question is will you survive without it? Try it—I dare you!

6. Rest through worship, both private and corporate.

What does this lengthy rant on the Sabbath have to do with the self-love ingredient of heart readiness for leadership in ministry? Simply this, without the rhythmic interruption of Sabbath rest, leaders are far more likely to succumb to the blurring influence of an ill-conceived self-identity.

We may even start believing some lies about our failures or, on the other hand, our indispensability. Sabbath rest affords us the time to be reminded of who God truly is. But it also provides opportunity for us to be reminded of who *we* are from God's perspective. Gordon T. Smith said it this way: "Work so easily becomes idolatrous, so easily that which defines us rather than being defined as children of God resting in God's salvation."[54] Sabbath is a time of disengagement both from the world and our ministry in order that we might enjoy deep rest and re-creation spiritually, emotionally, intellectually, and physically.

What can we, as leaders, do to help those we lead experience the joy of Sabbath rest and not see it as just another day or a boring day? Sabbath assumes a relationship, so whether it is our children in the home or members of the group we are privileged to lead, we must first of all pray for those people we are ministering to have a relationship with the Lord. Regardless of whether or not these people have a relationship with Christ, we as leaders must model what Sabbath rest looks like. One of the interesting aspects about the Jewish observance of Sabbath was that they did it as a family. Children knew they would have 100 percent of their dad without any interruption of work. It was a time when as family they turned their focus to what God had done for them—his completed work of deliverance. How are we doing, fellow Dad's?

In Summary

I want to make it very clear: I am not advocating a substitution of self-love for the enabling work of the Holy Spirit in an individual's life. As much as I have attempted to stress the critical importance of biblically informed self-love, I am not convinced that this fourth essential love is the panacea to all our spiritual, or emotional challenges; nor am I convinced it is a guarantee in and of itself to success or effectiveness in ministry leadership. However, an attenuated self-love, or one that is absent altogether, cannot help but undermine the effectiveness of any leader's ministry.

Effective leaders in ministry are people engaged in the process of learning to love themselves sincerely and biblically. They are those who have started to live their lives on the wavelength of Sabbath rest, whereby they consistently remind themselves that God is the one in control. They are people who are convinced that it is not their ministry or leadership

54. Smith, "Fostering Disengagement."

effectiveness that endears them to the heart of God, or by which they make the greatest contribution to the kingdom work of God. They are people who know that God's love for them cannot be enhanced or depleted in the least by anything they do or fail to do, and because of that, they can authentically love themselves.

For Group Discussion:

1. In this chapter, I made the following comment: "Put another way, wholesome self-love places us in the position of being able to receive either commendation or criticism in a manner that will nudge us closer to Christ and ultimately bring him glory." How do you respond to that statement?

2. In this chapter, I made the following statement regarding the way Christ followers have tended to gauge the importance of Sabbath rest: "We have completely ignored the Sabbath and in so doing have transformed it into meaninglessness on the misguided notion that it is solely associated with Old Testament law and is therefore unnecessary or unimportant through the grace of God in Christ. The intriguing thing to me is that the fourth commandment is the only one that we treat this way. We would never think of casting any of the other nine commandments in the same light!" Do you agree with this statement? If not, explain why. If so, why do you think it is so?

For Personal Reflection:

1. Reflect on a time when you received a compliment for something you did. How would you describe your response at the time? Try to recall what you said. Would you respond any differently today? If so, how and why?

2. Sondra Wheeler is cited in this chapter as saying, "justified criticism forces us to see ourselves differently, to incorporate new and unwelcome information into our understanding of who and what we are." Think of a time when you received some criticism. Was it justified? If so how did you handle or process that new and unwelcome information?

3. How would you gauge the degree to which you care for yourself physically? If improvement is needed, what would need to take place in order to make that happen?

Prayer: *Eternal God, Abba Father, how do I begin to thank you for the love you have extended to me? Thank you, oh Lord that my worth has nothing to do with accomplishment, that there is nothing I could do make you love me more or less. Thank you that I can love myself because of and through your grace. Forgive me for the times I neglect to care of myself or think too highly of myself. Keep my love for myself informed by the cross of Jesus for it's by his grace and for his glory that I pray these things, in Jesus' name. Amen.*

SIX

Selah: Leading with a Ready Heart

IN THE INTRODUCTION, I stated that this was a book about leadership and it was also a book about love. If you followed me carefully, you probably picked up on the sense that my intent here was not to provide insights to enhance growth and move the church forward numerically. Indeed, the intent of this book is based on the conviction that the hallmark of God's blessing is not discerned solely through an audit of attendance and finances.

Success is not our calling. Faithfulness is our calling; heart readiness is our calling. It is in this light that I say effectiveness in ministry leadership is not our responsibility. Effective ministry leadership is the fruit of indwelling spirit of the living Christ. A statement such as this may need some clarification in that it is quite evident that success or effectiveness in ministry leadership is in need of redefinition. Numerical growth *may* be indicative of effective leadership. Too often, though, it seems that is our default assumption. However, what if we were to define effectiveness in terms of our unapologetic, uncompromising faithfulness to the gospel, that is, the good news of God's provision for humanity's greatest need through the cross and resurrection of Christ? If we define effectiveness in this way, then we must be prepared for the likelihood that some, even many, will leave our churches. Both Peter and Paul remind us that Jesus and the message of the cross are likely to be offensive to many.[1] If we define success in terms of transformed lives that are dedicated to counter-cultural holiness and Christlikeness, we must not be alarmed if we find people drifting away quietly (or not so quietly) because many are of the mind that personal holiness resides in the private domain of the individual and should not be open to public assessment. Furthermore, a Christlike lifestyle will often

1. Rom 9:33; 1 Pet 2:8.

place a person in an unwelcomed, adversarial position that is contrary to the cultural ethos of the day. A wonderful aspect of the good news is that our sanctification, that is, our becoming more and more like Christ, is not something any Christ follower is capable of producing even through the most sincere and determined effort. Our personal holiness is possible only through the work of the Holy Spirit who translates the life of the living Christ in and through us. But that good news becomes bad news for those who want to retain control over their own lives, even their own sanctification. The old adage "God helps those who help themselves" simply cannot be sustained through Scripture. In fact the exact opposite comes to light through a careful reading of the Bible. It is better that we say, "God helps those who realize they are helpless!"

My purpose in carefully considering heart-readiness for leadership in ministry has not been to minimize the critical important skills and knowledge that a leader must possess. Scripture warns against placing a novice in the position of an overseer.[2] Nor has my intent been to launch the reader on a journey of inordinate introspection in regard to the more intangible heart issues of leadership. My intent here has been to underscore the vital tension that must exist between the heart and head of the leader. Furthermore, my intent here has been to demonstrate that heart readiness must be foundational to all knowledge and skills required of any leader in ministry. Leaders seldom if ever fail morally due to lack of knowledge or skill. That kind of shortcoming is always first and foremost an issue of the heart. This is why Solomon implored his son to "Keep your heart with all vigilance for from it flow the springs of life."[3] Staying true to this mandate can be particularly challenging when ministry is a grind and sin is annoyingly attractive.

The heart readiness we have explored in this book must never be seen or used as an excuse for passivity or a shabby work ethic. Scripture has nothing good to say about the lazy person and has much to say about the perils of being a sluggard. But by the same token, a frenetic, high octane lifestyle must never be allowed to excuse superficial heart readiness in relation to our love for the Word, for the church, for our neighbor, and for ourselves. As Mike Lueken has said: "This damages the soul. We can be highly effective Christian leaders but marginal Christ followers."[4] If our

2. 1 Tim 3:6.

3. Prov 4:23.

4. Carlson and Lueken, *Renovation*, 105.

desire is to lead people into a deeper experience of the four loves we have considered here, it behooves us as leaders to show the way through consistent personal example.

In Joshua 3 we have the account of Israel's amazing crossing of the Jordon River into the land that God had promised would be theirs. This event took place during harvest season when the Jordon overflowed its banks, presenting an even greater challenge to Joshua and the nation he was leading. For whatever reason, rather than simply causing a miraculous stoppage of the river, God determined that the priests, the spiritual leaders of the nation, had to get their feet into the water first.[5] God's plan was for the entire nation to cross that seasonally high and treacherous river, but the crossing began with the leadership. The only ones that got their feet wet in this miraculous crossing were the priests: "and as soon as those bearing the ark had come as far as the Jordon, and the feet of the priests bearing the ark were dipped in the brink of the water (now the Jordan overflows all its banks throughout the time of harvest . . .)"[6] As a result of their willingness to take that enormous risk, the entire nation was able to cross over "on dry ground."[7]

There are going to be times when those entrusted with the privilege and responsibility of leadership in ministry are going to be called to be the first to get their feet wet in what might seem to be a daunting challenge. Consistency in the four essential loves considered in this book is impossibly beyond the realm of sheer human effort. True heart readiness is possible only through the miraculous work of God's grace. But that grace remains inoperative as long as we stand on the shore waiting for God to do something in and through us or in the lives of others. Loving God with our whole being and the subsequent love of God's Word, the church, our neighbor, and ourselves all must begin with a conviction on the part of the leader that these four loves of heart readiness are essential to effective leadership in ministry.

The challenge in all of this is to maintain these four essential loves without allowing a subtle shift toward idolatry that places any one or more of them above our love for the Lord. That is precisely why we began with the foundational, wholehearted love for God in chapter one. Our love for God is where we find the headwaters from which all other loves flow; and

5. Josh 3:14–17.
6. Josh 3:15.
7. Josh 3:17.

those loves in turn provide the river on which skills and knowledge may be applied effectively through the life of the leader.

Over the past several decades numerous publications have identified and addressed a perceived crisis in leadership within the Christian church. We have discovered that there are several different leadership styles that not everyone responds to positively. We have also come to believe that effectiveness in leadership varies from culture to culture and from generation to generation. Many believe that the crisis in leadership revolves around the fact that for too long leadership has been almost the private reserve of the male gender, and that women have been precluded unnecessarily and unfortunately from key leadership positions. On the other hand, some believe that men have failed to step up and take leadership, thus leaving women no choice but to take on leadership that God never intended. In addition, leaders who have been found guilty of fraudulent practices and moral indiscretions (all of which the Bible calls, quite simply, sin!) have left millions disillusioned and unwilling to trust their leaders. Examples could be cited from presidents of world powers to pastors of churches to leaders of Boy Scout troops, and the list could go on.

Because of horrific choices leaders have made in the past, leaders today can no longer safely make assumptions regarding the attitudes of those they lead. *Holding office is no longer a guarantee of maintaining respect.* William Wells Brown, a nineteenth-century abolitionist, once said, "People don't follow titles, they follow courage."[8] Amending it slightly, I would say people are far more likely to follow a leader, not on the basis of his office or her title, but on the knowledge that their leader loves the right things in the right way and for the right reasons.

I have a very good, long-time friend who works as a captain on a Boeing 767 for Air Canada. Before he was ever permitted to take the controls and fly any aircraft full of passengers, he had to demonstrate, in clear and measurable ways, that he was ready. He had to demonstrate knowledge and skill in takeoff and landing procedures, as well as a variety of other scenarios. His readiness to fly is regularly and rigorously assessed. Heart readiness for ministry leadership is not as easy to gauge, but, I would argue, is as equally important.

Heart readiness never brings a leader to the point of having arrived, able to say, "I've made it!" Rather, like the apostle Paul, our goal is to be:

8. Wells Brown, online.

That I might know him and the power of his resurrection, and may share in his sufferings, becoming like him in his death, that by any means possible I may attain the resurrection from the dead. Not that I have already obtained this or am already perfect, but I press on to make it my own, because Christ Jesus made me his own. Brothers, I do not consider that I have made it my own. But one thing I do: forgetting what lies behind and straining forward to what lies ahead, I press on toward the goal for the prize of the upward call of God in Christ Jesus.[9]

A person whose heart is prepared for leadership is in process. This person recognizes how desperately she or he constantly is in need of God's grace, since even the ability to love God with our whole being and subsequently to love his Word, the church, the lost, and oneself is a gift of God's grace. Dallas Willard says it so well: "The great saints are not those who need *less* grace, but those who consume the most grace, who indeed are most in need of grace—those who are saturated by grace in every dimension of their being. Grace to them is like breath."[10] It is by God's grace alone that any of us are able to lead in ministry. It is by his grace that we are able to develop in heart readiness, in loving God with all we are, in loving his Word, his church, the lost, and ourselves. And doing so is solely by God's grace, and completely for God's glory!

9. Phil. 3:10–14.

10. Willard, *Renovation of the Heart*, 93–94.

Bibliography

Aldrich, Joe. *Lifestyle Evangelism*. Sisters, OR: Multnomah, 1983.

Barna, George. *Grow Your Church from the Outside In*. Ventura, CA: Regal, 2002.

Barth, Karl. *The Church and the Churches*. Grand Rapids, MI: William B. Eerdmans, 1936, 2005.

Benner, David G. *Spirituality and the Awakening Self*. Grand Rapids, MI: Brazos, 2012.

Bonhoeffer, Dietrich. "Loving our Enemies: A Sermon on Romans 12:16–21," translated by Evan Drake Howard. *The Reformed Journal*, April 1985, 18–21.

———, translated by John W. Doberstein, *Life Together*. New York: Harper & Row, 1954.

Bowman, Ray, and Eddy Hall. *When Not to Build*. Grand Rapids, MI: Baker, 2000.

Brown. Dan. *The Da Vinci Code*. New York: Doubleday, 2004.

Brownback, Paul. *The Danger of Self-Love*. Chicago: Moody, 1982.

Buchanan, Mark. *The Rest of God: Restoring Your Soul by Restoring Your Sabbath*. Nashville: W Publishing, 2006.

Buttrick, George Arthur. *The Interpreter's Bible, Volume 7*. Nashville: Abingdon, 1951.

Buttrick, David. *Homiletic: Moves and Structures*. Philadelphia, PA: Fortress, 1987.

Campolo, Tony, and Mary Albert Darling. *The God of Intimacy and Action*. San Francisco: Jossey-Bass, 2007.

Carlson, Kent, and Mike Lueken. *Renovation of the Church*. Downers Grove, IL: InterVarsity, 2011.

Calvin, John. *Institutes of the Christian Religion*. Grand Rapids, MI: William B. Eerdmans, 1995.

Chesterton, G. K. *Orthodoxy*. Wheaton, IL: Harold Shaw, 1994.

Conder, Tim. *The Church in Transition: The Journey of Existing Churches into the Emerging Culture*. Grand Rapids, MI: Zondervan, 2006.

Dawn, Marva J. *The Sense of Call: A Sabbath Way of Life for Those Who Serve God, the Church and the World*. Grand Rapids, MI: William B. Eerdmans, 2006.

Demarest, Bruce A. *Satisfy Your Soul: Restoring the Heart of Christian Spirituality*. Colorado Springs CO: Navpress, 1999.

DeYoung, Kevin, and Ted Kluck. *Why We Love the Church*. Chicago: Moody, 2009.

Dunham, Robert E. "Loving God with All Our Minds: A Reminder for Preachers." *Journal for Preachers*, Lent 2011, 19–24.

Erickson, Millard. *Christian Theology*. Grand Rapids, MI: Baker, 1985.

Estes, Steve. *Called to Die*. Grand Rapids, MI: Zondervan, 1986.

Ford, Leighton. *The Attentive Life*. Downers Grove, IL: InterVarsity, 2008.

Foster, Richard. *Celebration of Discipline*. Revised Edition. San Francisco: Harper & Row, 1988.

Galli, Mark. *Francis of Assisi and His World*. Downers Grove, IL: InterVarsity, 2002.

———. *"Speak* the Gospel." *Christianity Today*. Online: www.christianitytoday.com/ct/2009/mayweb-only/120–42.0.html

Giles, Kevin. *What on Earth Is the Church?* Downers Grove, IL: InterVarsity, 1995.

Greear, J. D. *Gospel: Rediscovering the Power that Made Christianity Revolutionary*. Nashville: B & H, 2011.

Grenz, Stanley J. *The Social God and the Relational Self: A Trinitarian Theology of the Imago Dei*. Louisville, KY: Westminster John Knox, 2001.

———. *Theology for the Community of God*. Grand Rapids, MI: William B. Eerdmans, 2000.

Grudem, Wayne. *Systematic Theology: An Introduction to Biblical Doctrine*. Grand Rapids, MI: Zondervan, 1994.

Herschel, Abraham Joshua. *The Sabbath: Its Meaning for Modern Man*. Boston: Shambhala, 2003.

Hoekema, Anthony. *The Christian Looks at Himself*. Grand Rapids, MI: William Eerdmans, 1975.

Howell, James C. *The Beauty of the Word*. Louisville, KY: Westminster John Knox, 2011.

Hungsberger, George R., and Craig Van Gelder. *The Church Between Gospel and Culture*. Grand Rapids, MI: W. B. Eerdmans, 1996.

Jantzen, Kyle. *Faith and Fatherland: Parish Politics in Hitler's Germany*. Minneapolis: Fortress, 2008.

Janzen, J. Gerald. "The Claim of the Shema." *Encounter* 59:1–2 1998, 243–57.

Jeanrond, Werner G. *A Theology of Love*. London: T & T Clark, 2010.

Kang, Joshua Choonmin. *Scripture by Heart: Devotional Practices for Memorizing God's Word*. Downers Grove, IL: InterVarsity, 2010.

Keller, Timothy. *Center Church: Doing Balanced Gospel-Centered Ministry in Your City*. Grand Rapids, MI: Zondervan, 2012.

———. *Counterfeit Gods*. New York: Dutton, 2009.

Kent, Michael R. *Falling in Love with Yourself*. New York: Paulist, 1994.

Kierkegaard, Soren. *Works of Love*. New York: Harper, 2009

Kimball, Dan. *The Emerging Church*. Grand Rapids, MI: Zondervan, 2003.

Krishnan, Sunder. *Loving God with All You've Got*. Camp Hill, PA: Wingspread, 2003.

Lewis, C. S. *The Four Loves*. London: Geoffrey Bles, 1960.

Mahaney, C. J. "The Atonement." Online: www.youtube.com/watch?v=q8lA47X4G8s, accessed December 7, 2012.

McAlpine, Campbell. *Alone with God: A Manual of Biblical Meditation*. Minneapolis: Bethany Fellowship, 1981.

McAlpine, William R. "Biblical Illiteracy and the Technological Tsunami." *CM Alliance*. ca, Fall 2012, 16–20.

———. *Sacred Space for the Missional Church: Engaging Culture through the Built Environment*. Eugene, OR: Wipf & Stock, 2011.

McBride, S. Dean, Jr. "The Yoke of the Kingdom: An Exposition of Deuteronomy 6:4–5." *Interpretation* Vol 27, No. 3 (July 1973), 273–306.

McCracken, Brett. *Hipster Christianity: When Church and Cool Collide*. Grand Rapids, MI: Baker, 2010.

McKenna, David L. *The Communicator's Commentary Series Volume 2: Mark*. Waco, TX: Word Books, 1982.

McKnight, Scot. *The Jesus Creed*. Brewster, MA: Paraclete, 2007.

McNeal, Reggie. *A Work of Heart: Understanding How God Shapes Spiritual Leaders*. San Francisco: Jossey-Bass, 2000.

McQuilkin, Robertson. "Living by Vows." *Christianity Today*, October 8, 1990, 38–40.

Montag, Christian, et al. "Internet Addiction and Personality in First-person Shooter Video Gamers." *Journal of Media Psychology*, 2011; Vol. 23(4):163–173.

Newbegin, Lesslie. *Foolishness to the Greeks*. Grand Rapids, MI: William B. Eerdmans, 1986.

———. *The Household of God*. London: Paternoster, 1998.

Oakland, Roger. *Faith Undone*. Silverton, OR: Lighthouse Trails, 2007.

Oden, Thomas C. *Life in the Spirit: Systematic Theology: Volume Three*. Peabody, MA: Prince Press, 2001.

Osborne, Cecil G. *The Art of Learning to Love Yourself*. Grand Rapids, MI: Zondervan, 1976.

Peterson, Eugene H. *The Message*. Colorado Springs, CO: NavPress, 2002.

———. *Under the Unpredictable Plant*. Grand Rapids, MI: William B. Eerdmans, 1994.

Piper, John. "Self-love and the Christian Counselor's Task." *Reformed Journal*, May, 1978, 13–18.

Price, Chris. "Love the Groom, Hate the Bride," *Grounded* (blog), www. groundedinthegospel.com/blog/love-the-groom-hate-the-bride.

Reeves, Kevin. *The Other Side of the River*. Silverton, OR: Lighthouse Trails, 2007.

Sanders, J. Oswald. *Spiritual Leadership*. (Second Revision) Chicago: Moody, 1994.

Scheaffer, Francis. *The Church at the End of the 20th Century*. Westchester, IL: Crossway, 1985.

———. *The Mark of the Christian*. Downers Grove, IL: InterVarsity, 1974.

———. *No Final Conflict*. Downers Grove, IL: InterVarsity, 1976.

Sheehan, Thomas. *The First Coming: How the Kingdom of God Became Christianity*. New York: Random House, 1986.

Smith, Gordon T. *Essential Spirituality*. Nashville: Thomas Nelson, 1994.

———. "Fostering Disengagement With the World—Sabbath." Global Vault website, www.vimeo.com/27748093?action=share.Stott, John R. W. *Christian Mission: What the Church Should Be Doing Now!* Downers Grove, IL: InterVarsity, 1975.

———. *The Living Church*. Downers Grove, IL: InterVarsity, 2007.

Swete, Henry Barclay. *Commentary on Mark*. Grand Rapids, MI: Kregel, 1977.

Tan, Kim Huat. "The Shema and Early Christianity." *Tyndale Bulletin* Vol. 59, No. 2, 2008, 181–206.

Taylor, W. David O., editor. *For the Beauty of the Church*. Grand Rapids, MI: Baker, 2010.

Toronto, Ellen. "Time Out of Mind: Dissociation in the Virtual World." *Psychoanalytic Psychology*, Vol. 26, No. 2, 117–33.

Tournier, Paul. *A Place for You: Psychology and Religion*. New York: Harper & Row, 1968.

Trobisch, Walter. *Love Yourself*. Downers Grove, IL: InterVarsity, 1976.

Van Gelder, Craig. *The Essence of the Church: A Community Created by the Spirit*. Grand Rapids, IL: Baker, 2000.

———. *The Ministry of the Missional Church*. Grand Rapids, MI: Baker, 2007.

———, editor. *The Missional Church & Denominations*. Grand Rapids, MI: William B. Eerdmans, 2008.

Bibliography

Viola, Frank, and George Barna. *Pagan Christianity?: Exploring the Roots of Our Church Practices*. Barna, 2008.

Volf, Miroslav. *Captive to the Word of God: Engaging the Scriptures for Contemporary Theological Reflection*. Grand Rapids, MI: William B. Eerdmans, 2010.

Weaver, Darlene Fozard. *Self-Love & Christian Ethics*. Cambridge, MA: Cambridge University Press, 2002.

Wells Brown, William. Quotes Museum. Online: www.quotes-museum.com/author/William_Wells_Brown.

Wesley, John. *The Works of John Wesley*, Vol. 5. Nashville TN: Abingdon, 1984.

Wessel, Walter W. "Mark" in *The Expositor's Bible Commentary, Volume 8*. Grand Rapids, MI: Regency Reference Library, 1984.

Wheeler, Sondra. *What We Were Made For: Christian Reflections on Love*. San Francisco: Jossey-Bass, 2007.

White, James Emery. *A Mind for God*. Downers Grove, IL: InterVarsity, 2006.

Willard, Dallas. *The Divine Conspiracy*. San Francisco: Harper, 1997.

———. *Renovation of the Heart*. Colorado Springs, CO: NavPress, 2002.

Wilson, Jonathan R. *Why Church Matters: Worship, Ministry, and Mission in Practice*. Grand Rapids, MI: Brazos, 2006.

Wright, N. T. *Surprised by Hope*. New York: Harper One, 2008.

Yoder, Perry B., editor. *Take this Word to Heart: The Shema in Torah and Gospel*. Elkhart: Institute of Mennonite Studies, 2005.

Zacharias, Ravi. *Recapture the Wonder*. Nashville: Integrity, 2003.

Zachman, Randall C. "'Deny Yourself and Take up Your Cross': John Calvin on the Christian Life." *International Journal of Systematic Theology*. Vol 11, No. 4 October 2009, 466–82.